# WILFRED GRENFELL

OTHER BIOGRAPHIES BY BASIL MILLER

# WILFRED GRENFELL

*Labrador's Dogsled Doctor*

*Basil Miller*

Zondervan Publishing House
GRAND RAPIDS, MICHIGAN

# CONTENTS

# Chapter 1

# THE CALL OF ADVENTURE

HE DID NOT WISH for the life of an Alexander, a Caesar or Napoleon, a Croesus or Midas, a Voltaire or Rousseau. To Wilfred Grenfell, the wealth of Herod or the learning of the philosophers was relatively insignificant. He scaled his life so that when posterity read the records of his achievements, it could say, "His was a replica of the Master's spirit."

He threw the spotlight of exploration and civilization upon one of the bleakest shores lapped by the seas and one of earth's most passed-by regions. By the time he was laid to rest in Mother Earth's bosom, Labrador was as well-known as Broadway, and civilization was conscious that through serving Christ, Wilfred Grenfell had remade a people long forgotten.

Wilfred was cradled in a land ideally situated to spark into being the embers which were to find their full blaze in the Labradorian wilderness. The last day of February, 1865, Algernon Grenfell, headmaster of the Mostyn House School, located in Parkgate, England, on the banks of the River Dee, little dreamed when the doctor handed him the latest addition to his family that the baby whom he christened Wilfred should become one of time's greatest

7

sons. The school which he had purchased from a great-
uncle was housed in an old stagecoach inn, and many were
the tales which little Wilfred was to hear about the
cousins who had stayed at the inn when the coaches swung
through Parkgate from London on their way to the Irish
Sea.

Those days, when Wilfred's childish feet scuffed along
the rough inn-turned-school floors, had passed, and the
once greatly blessed Parkgate had slipped into the nodding
condition of a sleepy little country village. The railroad
trains puffed their way through the town where once
the prancing coach horses had stamped, and Wilfred
sought on the Irish Sea the excitement which his boyish
nature craved.

Father Algernon, a man of high scholarly attainments
and a Fellow of the Royal Geographic Society, took great
care of Wilfred's early schooling, and wished for his son
a higher fame than he himself had been able to attain.
Though a student at Balliol, illness had compelled him
to leave the university before he completed his course.
Many were the times when he read Greek and Latin
classics to his son and the other students at the school, and
he conversed with them fluently in French and German.

He was a man of no mean mental stature, and enjoyed
an enviable reputation as a geologist. The growing son
held his father in high esteem, and years later, when
writing the story of his pilgrimage through life, Wilfred,
in autobiographical reminiscences, looked upon his father
as "most generous and softhearted, who never refused us
any reasonable request, and very few unreasonable ones."
He allowed the lad and his brothers a large "amount of
self-determination enjoyed by few."

The adventurous boy never tired of hearing his father
tell of the Grenfell forebears who had gone to sea,
and there achieved fame, if not fortune, living their lives
in the wild way of seafarers. They hailed from Cornwall

and the West Country and in the days gone by had sailed the Spanish Main. The names of Basil Grenfell, spelled in those days "Grenville," Sir Richard Grenfell and John Pascoe Grenfell had come down in history as symbolic of valiant deeds in battle, and they charged through Wilfred's mind with the tread of an army.

Prophetic was the fact, if Wilfred then had known it, that the first English vessel which sailed for Newfoundland was called the *Grenfell*, for here later the lad-grown-to-be-a-man was to build his career as the Doctor of Labrador.

Nor were the tales his mother told him of her lineage less thrilling to the lad than those with which his father held him spellbound when he and his beautiful wife were in a story-swapping mood. Wilfred's mother was the daughter of an English army colonel, in India, where a brother was the engineer officer at the seige of Lucknow until Havelock finally arrived to take over command. Many members of her family were in military service in India.

Wilfred was blessed with three brothers. one of whom died when seven. The remaining trio—Algernon, the oldest, Wilfred, the next oldest, and Cecil, five years younger, spent many glorious childhood and youth days together in this sleepy little land that edged the Irish Sea. Holidays, when the boarding boys left the Grenfell school, were times of joyous companionship for Wilfred and his older brother.

School out, into the "sands of Dee," made famous by their poet-cousin Charles Kingsley, the boys raced. To the south across the estuary, flowing into the Irish Sea, Wales beckoned. Building a boat of their own, the two boys explored every nook and corner of the shore, nosing their craft into each channel and salt-water runnel that cut deep into the sand banks.

The main channel, narrow and rapid, was whipped by a raging current, and challenged young Wilfred's adventurous spirit. Often into this, called the Deep, the lad threw himself, and was carried by the currents to the opposite Welsh shore, where he would drift along until at length he came to the Great Cop. Here he stopped to investigate the embarkment, started but never finished, intended to tie together the English and Welsh shores.

Farther afield, up the Dee, were great salt marshes which fascinated young Wilfred. Here he began his life of exploration which was to urge him through the Labradorian wildness. Nor could he erase from memory the tang and lure of the sea, nor the pounding of the surf, nor the boom of the storm-whipped billows. He grew up amid fleets of fishing ships, and fisher folks were a part of his early background. As a little boy he had toddled into their homes, and when, later, God's call to service rang loudly in his soul, it is fitting that the lot of fishermen on the bleak Labradorian coast should be bettered by his talents.

Everywhere he and his brothers went they found thousands of birds—sandpipers, oyster catchers, plovers, dunlins, ducks, terns, curlews-and on their homeward trips, by boat or afoot, they often bagged their evening meal. The lad, growing into youthhood, was thus as much at home on water as on land, and he became an expert swimmer, a good marksman, and a sturdy walker. All of this was to be excellent training for his future when he gave his heart to Labrador.

Early Wilfred's collector's urge began to assert itself, and he started his own private museum, which, as time went on, became the center of his father's Mostyn House School's museum. From an old village sailor he learned how to skin, stuff and mount birds, and his specimens were a credit to anyone. To these he added trophies, sent from relatives in India, which were mounted and hung on the walls of his home. Birds, moths, butterflies and wild flowers also took their places with the animals.

Often during school holidays, his father and mother would go to the Continent for their vacation, leaving Wilfred and his brothers in care of a school matron. Then adventure-loving Wilfred, finding himself free to do as he pleased, raced to the sea or the river, the dunes or the salt marshes. On one occasion the boys wired a cousin in London, saying, "Come down and stay the holidays. Father has gone to Aix."

"Not gone yet. Father," was the answer.

However, the cousin arrived a few days later, and a joyous holiday was spent by the four.

Carefree days soon passed and Father Grenfell gave his time to selecting a suitable university preparatory school for Wilfred, realizing that the brilliant son held the possibilities of a high future. The selection finally was Marlborough, a school of about six hundred resident boys, where Wilfred was matriculated at fourteen. Situated near Savernake Forest in Wiltshire, one of England's loveliest countries, the lad found much to his delight, and as he roamed through the college buildings—in England, university preparatory schools were called colleges—they brought back nostalgic memories of dear Mostyn. Here, too, had been a fine old inn in stagecoach days, though grander than the one at Parkgate.

When he first arrived he admired the high gates marking the entrance, and the long avenue of graceful trees leading to the main building. To one side of this he found other buildings serving as schoolrooms, dining hall, chapel and residences. Farther afield were the recreational grounds, where he was soon to surpass in athletics.

Nor was his scholastic ability belatedly recognized, for during the first term he won a scholarship. His long hair did not in the least endear him to the other pupils, for this, plus his belligerent disposition, caused him to be known as the "Beast." Leaving Mostyn, he had not left behind his love for collecting specimens and often, quite contrary to the school rules, he crept at night into the near-by Savernake Forest, where, with a small lantern and a butterfly net, he caught moths.

The call of the water lured him to the Kennett River, where he swam whenever the weather permitted. He was challenged by the school athletics, at which he excelled, but he could not overcome a tendency to play pranks on the other scholars. He rushed tardily to chapel—for which often he suffered what seemed to be dire penalties—and he built up many techniques by which he might escape unpleasant school duties.

Although unaware of it at the time, he was living his future theory of education, for he viewed school training as enabling one to correspond most completely to his environment, to develop a healthy body and primarily a culture "of the spirit which makes living to serve the world the first objective." He felt in his maturer years that turning knowledge "into service alone justifies the toil spent to achieve it," and adds the true value of laboring joyously in a chosen field of Christian endeavor.

After two years spent at the school, during which time a persistent cough had forced Wilfred to endure tedious days at the infirmary, the resident physician, called Dr. Fungi—a perversion by the scholars of "Dr. Fergus"—diagnosed the difficulty as lung congestion or tuberculosis and ordered him to southern France for the winter. Despite the seriousness of the malady, this was glad news to the lad, for he remembered the stories his father and mother had told him of an aunt living at Hyeres in a glorious villa, high-perched on a hill and overlooking the sea.

Here, after a most exciting journey, his first trip out of native England, he was welcomed by his relative. Nor was the sixteen-year-old youth displeased when he met the two delightful and athletic daughters of the aunt's widowed friend who shared the joys of the villa with her. Wilfred found this a storybook visit, for years later, remembering those long-ago days, he called them "a winter spent in paradise."

Nor did he find it boring to follow the doctor's orders to spend as much time out of doors as possible. The vivacious girls took their friend in tow, and together they tramped the hills. Here they netted butterflies, caught frogs, collected trap-door spiders and many other zoological and "bugological" specimens which became welcome additions at the boy's growing museum.

His pleasures, enjoyed in the company of two lovely lassies, were not limited to capturing bugs, for the sea called, and the three spent long hours swimming in the warm water. They rode horseback over the hilly trails that led to the heights where vision-luring vistas entrapped Wilfred's adventurous mind. One unforgettable day they visited a carnival at Nice.

These days of high adventure were specked by the flies of irritation in the form of a tutor whom school-headmaster Mr. Grenfell furnished. He came with orders to cram Wilfred's head with mathematics, and to saturate him with Latin and French literature. Wilfred, looking back upon the tutor's contribution to his youthful scholarship, decided that it consisted mainly in giving him a more-than-nodding familiarity with the fables of La Fontaine, which he promptly memorized, and a firsthand knowledge of the many lizards which raced along the walls of the tutor's garden.

The winter was well spent from the lad's viewpoint, despite the fact that the tutor had dampened his enthusiasm, and was more than worth the price in renewed health and energy.

Returning to the college, from which he had been

sent to France, he continued his studies. During this time
he was greatly impressed by a kindly act of his mother's.
The boys at the school took pride in being well dressed on
Sundays, which was called "good form." This implied
wearing a buttonhole flower at morning chapel. To make
this possible his mother mailed him a little box of flowers
every week. The fact that she picked them with her own
hands made them unspeakably precious to her son.

Looking back at his mother's gracious concern for him,
years later he declared that the act was not waste of energy,
for the raising of flowers became a lifetime hobby, and
he never lost pride in his appearance. He was also careful
to avoid mental and spiritual sloppiness. How he treasured
those little love-messages from the dearest companion he
had on earth.

These deeds of love, "not words, never faded from my
soul, and made their appeal to the wandering boy to 'arise
and do things,'" he says.

Speaking of his mother later, he tells of discovering
among her effects a book which, next to her Bible, he
valued most highly. This was the ledger book of the school,
which she kept meticulously through the years, despite the
financial caprices of her family.

When, in later years, the Labradorian doctor discovered
the faithful record of her stewardship through the passing
years, "during which we had taken everything for granted,
and without gratitude accepted all that we wanted. Here
was the record, during many long years, of endless and
arduous tasks, the most monotonous, and all achieved
for us." When he looked at the rows upon rows of figures,
page after page, neat and carefully entered, and patiently
analyzed and balanced, "in the handwriting so dear to my
heart, a new light seemed to shine on me, showing a great
deal more of the meaning of Christ to me in my normal
boyhood than I had been conscious of."

Schooldays were racing to a close, and changes were disrupting the family routine. In 1883, when Wilfred was eighteen, Father Algernon felt the call to devote himself to religious work, and giving up his teaching, he accepted the chaplaincy of the large London Hospital. Talking with his son concerning the future, he inquired what the young man wanted to do in life.

Young Wilfred until then had given no serious consideration to this problem, a problem soon to become vexing. To him, life seemed to flow endlessly by. His father and mother furnished the means for travel, bug-catching and bird-stuffing, college and clothes, without his having to give any attention to such worldly details. But now, for the first time, Wilfred faced the great doors which opened upon life, and as he looked at them, he wondered what was to be found on the other side.

Said Algernon to his son, "Go to the minister for advice."

Wilfred had viewed pleasures as his rightful portion. He had seen little of poverty and felt none of its pinch, and now to face the thought that he must make his own way in life was not easy. Those stirring tales, told by Mother Grenfell, of relatives in India, living, fighting, and enjoying the thrills of that colorful land, had made him think for a while that theirs might be a pleasant mode of living. The idea stopped shortly there.

Rather than going to the minister, a friend, the wife of a missionary to India, was living near by, and Wilfred decided to interview her. She soon disabused his mind of the alluring idea that tiger hunting was a self-supporting trade. Said the missionary, the desire welling from her service-filled heart, "Become a clergyman . . ."

But there was no fire in the thought, and as he mused upon it, the flames of desire embered lower until they flickered and died.

His father came forward with the suggestion that he consult the family physician, a man with a wide practice, whom the Grenfells respected highly. The old physician showed Grenfell a preserved human brain. The experience was new, and one significant for the future. He had stuffed birds and preserved bugs, trailed lizards to their lair, shot ducks and studied them, but the sight of a human brain was an experience he would never forget.

He thrilled at the surge of new emotions within him. He had never thought of man's body as a machine, and to see this white of matter that controlled physical strength and growth and the marvelous mental and spiritual responses to life, became an amazing experience, a soul-exciting moment.

When he told his father of the incident, the older man knew that the son had at last found his true interest, and he suggested that he either enter Oxford, where his older brother had just matriculated, or "come with me to London and begin work in the London Hospital and University with the view of becoming a doctor."

At that moment the famous Dr. Grenfell of Labrador was in the making, and the hand of God was upon the decision, shaping the young man's future, molding his capacities, and preparing him for the mighty feats of spiritual valor that were later to mark his life, though of course Wilfred was totally ignorant of the future which loomed upon his tomorrows. Immediately he began the necessary studies for entrance examinations, which he passed acceptably.

Here he found many new subjects of study of which he had been totally ignorant—subjects such as botany, zoology, physics, physiology, comparative anatomy. In fact, so new were the courses at the medical school that his previous education, except for the fact that it conditioned him for further study, was of relatively little value.

The medical school he attended was attached to the London Hospital, England's largest, and was well located for practical purposes in the city's poorest section on the famous Whitechapel Road. The hospital had more than nine hundred beds that were always full, with patients waiting for every vacancy, and it furnished a challenging field for clinical work and practical experience in contact with an unbelievably wide range of diseases.

Wilfred found the teaching exceedingly mediocre, but looking back upon it from the vantage point of later years, he was grateful for it. It was usually necessary to sign up for the privilege of attending lectures, but he discovered that by tipping the record-keeper, one might skip even the necessity of class attendance, and instruction, usually presented in the form of lectures. In his entire course, he was present at only two botany classes. In physiology, for instance, there was no apparatus with which to verify teaching or illustrate the human form.

Chemistry was a chaos of irrelevant facts, and other studies were similar. He found the dispensary useless from the point of view of practical experience received, for his sole achievement was the making of eggnogs.

Despite poor teaching, he was able to pass the examinations at the College of Physicians and Surgeons and at the London University. His Labradorian work shows that, strangely enough, he possessed both skill and knowledge.

During his medical-student days he rowed in the inter-hospital races and played on the football team. He was secretary of cricket, football and rowing clubs, and he won the inter-hospital football cup. He threw the hammer in the united hospitals' sports, and won second place for two years. So thoroughly did he enjoy athletics and so keenly was he interested in them that he devoted all his spare time to their constructive program of body-building.

Here again the hand of God was guiding him, for in the great adventure which awaited him in Labrador would demand a strong and supple body, one to withstand the rigors of fifty degrees below zero, days spent on dogsled trails, and privations almost beggaring description.

At this stage of his career he was still a happy-go-lucky Grenfell, dreaming of his seafaring ancestors' prowess, and living in imagination with his India relatives who spent their time between battles and skirmishes in tiger-hunting and dozing in the sun. He looked upon his vocation with anticipation, but viewed it complacently as requiring no more of him than was expected from any English gentleman with a profession.

God, however, was working silently but steadily, and the act of merely stopping to listen for the moment at an evangelistic meeting changed the current of his life.

# Chapter 2

# THE PLEA OF THE FISHER FOLK

GOD WAS TO ACCOMPLISH great things through this Wilfred Grenfell, now on his way to becoming a doctor. But first he must experience a mighty spiritual transformation. Wilfred's basic human capacities, his adventurous spirit, his virile imagination, his scalpel-keen mind and boundless physical energy fitted him especially for the divine task.

But God does not use men who have not been transformed by Christ, however extensive their culture, impressive their attainments, or superb their physical equipment. He uses only thoroughly consecrated men who will heed the Divine Voice for guidance and grasp the Divine Hand for encouragement.

The instrument for this soul-transformation was close at hand. Until now, Wilfred's background had been void of intense spiritual forces, for he lived in a shallow-water religious environment. He took religion as of the Church, and was a total stranger to the power of the Gospel. Men, God-used, are always born-again men, and until Grenfell had experienced this soul-altering change in his life, he was to remain unknown and unused. But once God converted him, there were challenging fields to explore, and a land to bring under the Gospel's power.

19

Young Grenfell, now in his twentieth year, was nearing the most auspicious time of his career. Moody and Sankey were in London holding a revival, the glory of which reaches the farest ends of eternity.

One night in 1885, during his hospital trainee days, where he was still receiving classroom work instruction, he was sent on an outpatient sick call, a mission which led him through Shadwell to a poorer district of the city. There was never a dearth of these patients, for one of his duties was caring for those who were unable to secure their own doctor.

Completing the call, Wilfred, his little black satchel in hand, decided to return through Shadwell by a route unfamiliar to him. On his way through the section he came upon what appeared to be a huge circus tent. Being of a curious and adventuresome nature, he was drawn to join the crowd which loitered around the entrance.

God directed his feet to this particular tent on this occasion, and edging his way through the throng, he stood within the tent, where he saw a large crowd gathered, their heads bowed in prayer, while an old man on the platform led them to the throne by what the doctor thought to be a most circuitous route. The verbose brother seemed unable to locate the terminal facilities of the prayer, and Grenfell, tiring of the wordy barrage, turned on his heel and decided to go back to the hospital. Suddenly a commotion took place on the platform, and a large man leaped to his feet and said, "Let us sing a song while our brother finishes his prayer."

The doctor's curiosity was so aroused that he decided to remain and see what happened next. The unconventional character of the act appealed to the youth, who refused to be standardized by conventions and customs. While he listened to the music, his heart was touched, for soon another man arose and directed the congregation. When

the singing was finished, the first man took charge and
delivered a straight-from-the-heart message on salvation.

Grenfell found himself in a Moody-Sankey revival, and
as the famous evangelist, who during the course of his life
prayed personally at his altars with more than seven
hundred and fifty thousand seekers, preached Christ and
Him crucified in a sincere and personal manner, the doctor yearned for the Christ of whom the evangelist spoke.

"I did not know anything about the man," he says, in
telling, as he often did, the story of his conversion, "nor
did I see him again till fourteen years later. But he left
a new idea in my mind, the idea that loyalty to a living
leader was religion, and that knightly service in the
humblest life was an expression of it . . .

"Religion was chivalry, not an insurance ticket. Life
was a field of honor calling for courage to face it, not
a tragedy to escape from. What Christ asked us for was
reasonable service, or the service of our reason, but real,
hard service either way. His religion was a challenge . . .
The whole talk was of a living Leader of men."

Until now, religion in Wilfred's life had failed to take
on this element of challenge. It had been a normal part
of his background, a loving human religion practiced by
father and mother, but conventional withal, without the
stirring element of salvation from sin and the need for
being born again which was stressed in Moody's sermon.
Hitherto he had found nothing to inflame his spirit with
a passionate longing to do something for someone else, to
spend himself in service under the leadership of this
living Leader of men. His conversion, therefore, gave him
not only a totally new viewpoint, but as he accepted Christ
as His personal Redeemer, the step also wrought a spiritual
transformation. He had met the Man of Galilee, who
henceforth was to be Master of his career.

As he left the meeting, someone handed him Moody's
book *How To Read the Bible*. Taking this to the hospital

with him, he carefully studied it in the hours when he
was not preparing for his final examinations.  Suddenly
he saw life as an opportunity to accept the Master's challenge, "Go . . . preach . . . teach . . ."  The Bible became
his guide book.

The fledgling doctor was a new man.  His intellect had
been challenged, his outlook reslanted, his life energized
by Christ's coming into his heart.

While the flame of spiritual enthusiasm burned high,
a group of famous athletes who had given themselves to
Christ came to London to hold religious meetings.  Among
them were crack cricket players, oarsmen and others of
national and even international repute.  Being an athlete
himself, Grenfell found that they struck a responsive
chord in his heart, and he attended the meetings.

At the close of a service, the speaker of the evening urged
all who had made a decision to follow Christ to stand.
Grenfell, who until now had not had an occasion to testify
for Christ, noticed that in the front seats were sailors from
a ship in the Thames.  He watched as one of the boys, a
slight lad, stood courageously, while the others watched
with astonishment.  Chained by invisible forces to his
seat, the young doctor sat still, his face burning with the
thought of what his fellow medics, present with him,
would think if he, too, stood up for Jesus.

The sailor lad's brave act touched Grenfell's wavering
spirit, bolstered his morale, and he, too, leaped to his
feet.  Immediately he was flooded with a sense of spiritual
satisfaction and assurance, and of having found his place
in God's plan.  Now he felt that he must prove himself
worthy of this silent testimony.

After the meeting he experienced a richer, fuller sense
of Christ's nearness and his own spiritual transformation
than he had when he walked out of the tent.

This new consciousness of Christ's presence in his soul
must find an outlet in service.  He could no longer dam

up the power that had been released from the heavenly reservoirs. It must course through his being and water with spiritual hope and life the wastelands of humanity. Since his conversion in Moody's meeting, his parents had noticed the change in his life, especially his interest in evening prayers and Bible reading.

His mother, noticing Wilfred's intense desire to serve his Saviour, suggested to her son that he ask the Episcopal minister of the church she attended, if there was something he could do in the sphere of Christian service. At once the rector offered him the opportunity to teach a class of small boys in the Sunday school. Wilfred found them to be slum lads from the districts roundabout, and at once he found that Sunday school had little if any attraction for them.

Sometimes their antics were such as to drive the young doctor nearly to distraction. Nevertheless they continued to attend, finding something in the doctor's instruction or personality which lured them back to the class. Soon a deep affection arose between Grenfell and his pupils, due possibly to the boys' admiration of their teacher's athletic prowess. They discovered that he could outswim, outbox and outbowl any of them, and on the cricket field they were no match for him. He was the best football player they had ever met.

The doctor decided that he must combine religious instruction with physical activity in reaching these lads from the slums, so he taught them swimming in Victoria Park Lake. When he discovered that the lake was exceedingly, and hence unpleasantly, muddy late in the evening, since many had used it, he suggested that they swim early in the morning. Many were the times the lads scaled the gates and were heartily enjoying their swim when the gate-opener arrived.

He also added a sports program to his course of religious instruction. In the dining room of his boarding house he set up a boxing arena and equipped it for parallel-bar work. He desired to add other sports, but the small space available made this impossible. In all this his one desire was to teach the boys fair play, how to take defeat as men and how to be happy in victory.

Consequently, the lads began bringing their friends to these sports events, friends which the Sunday-morning class program could never lure into the church. Gradually they were being added to the class groups, but the short-sighted minister—bound by custom and chained to codes—decided that he could not approve the direction in which Grenfell was slanting the group's activities, and forthwith asked for Wilfred's resignation.

This, however, was a move in the right direction, for God had greater things for Grenfell to achieve, and into the new field He moved the young doctor. A fellow medical student, who held services on Sunday nights among underground lodging houses in a slum district, asked his companion to assist in the venture. Together with his co-worker he purchased a portable organ and began the new work, and the lodgers enjoyed the music if nothing else. Here for the first time he came in touch with genuine poverty, poverty which made life merely a scramble for existence, and often the young doctor found those who wished that life would end.

This was a new experience for Wilfred, for whom life had been comfortable and happy. Here also he met the trickster, the hypocrite and the cheater, who taught him the needed lesson that he must become hardened to fictitious tales of ill luck, persecution and "I'm temporarily out of funds." All this was in the divine pattern for Grenfell's life in Labrador.

When his Sunday-school class was disbanded, he joined his medical friend in conducting on Sundays what was then called a "ragged school," whose students were street waifs, as untamed as the wolves he was to encounter in

Labrador. He learned, to his sorrow, that they stole anything left in the building, and their sticky fingers soon seized anything movable. When a boy proved so annoying that he had to be thrown out, he retaliated by smattering the teachers with mud or pelting them with stones.

Temperance, a benefit from his interest in athletics, proved a heavy interest during these times, for he had learned on the football or cricket field the drinker was always the loser, and often the saloon keepers and their inebriated customers attacked him. All of this was but part of his divinely-shaped education which was forming his character into God's pattern for his future.

When vacation time arrived, Wilfred and his older brother rented a fishing boat and sailed from Anglesey into the Irish Sea. Totally indifferent to their destination, they permitted the winds to scud them along at the will of the summer breezes. Sometimes young Grenfell invited a medical classmate or two to enjoy the holiday. Many were their narrow escapes, but the casualties were few. In this manner Wilfred passed the holidays and learned much about the country's west coast. Often he and his friends visited the fishing villages and the little harbors where the fisher folk plied their trade.

This, too, was preparation for the time when he would sail the wide seas along the Newfoundland coasts.

Never completely happy when sailing alone, he began inviting members of his Sunday school and ragged school classes to enjoy the thrills of the sea with him. One summer thirteen companions went with him, taking all the necessary camping equipment—tents, sleeping needs, cooking apparatus. Along shore they camped, boated, swam and fished.

So successful were these trips that each summer more boys were included, until the number was near a hundred. During his final medical years at medical school, since he could not be absent from London for a long period, a friend permitted Grenfell to camp for the summer with his boys on the ground of his estate Lulworth Castle, which is near the sea.

Gradually the group assumed the form of a semi-military organization. The delightful grounds of the old estate, one of the most beautiful along the English coast, fascinated Grenfell no less than the lads. The property owner added to the zest of the vacation by giving a regatta and a picnic for the city boys.

On these trips the lads' spiritual skyline lifted, and they had visions of life's true meaning, visions which would never have come to them in the London slums. Here also the doctor gained many useful experiences and learned lessons for beyond the scope of his hospital life. These lessons were to prove useful in saving time in handling the knotty problems and the vexing people of Labrador.

Schooldays were about to be terminated, and the doctor would be ready to hang out his shingle: *Wilfred Grenfell, M. D., Physician and Surgeon.* In 1886, Wilfred, a nimble-brained student, passed his final examinations and became a full-fledged doctor. He was also inducted as a full member into the College of Physicians and the Royal College of Surgeons of England.

While at the hospital, he came into contact with numerous fishermen from the North Sea fleet, men who virtually lived on the water, spending possibly one in seven or ten days on shore. He learned first-hand from them the rigors of their work and the hazardous nature of their means of making a living. Their boats, they told him, were small, and as the gales of the North Sea swept with an icy breath across them, they were tossed about mercilessly. Often the men had to be lashed to their posts, and many times, so they told the kindly young doctor who attended them, their bones were snapped, their backs broken, and their flesh torn.

While listening to the stories these fishermen told him,

Grenfell was also attending the lectures on anatomy and surgery presented by Sir Frederick Treves, a noted Christian physician, who was deeply interested in these fishing sailors. Often Treves himself sailed with the fishing boats, crossed the Channel to Calais in a sailing lugger and made trips among the fleet. The famous doctor became interested in the young and brilliant student, and the friendship matured with the years. He also insisted that his students know what they were about, and know in what direction they were traveling toward their future.

Since Grenfell had accepted Christ, he was constantly examining the direction of his life, and gradually he asked himself, "Whither bound?"

One day Sir Frederick came to Wilfred with the suggestion that he go out with the fishing fleet.

"They need a doctor among them," he told the student. "Someone who can give them medicine, take care of their wounds, and give them a word as to their soul's welfare. Go and have a look at it."

Then he went on to explain how some Christian men had organized the Mission to Deep Sea Fishermen, had chartered a small vessel, and were sending it to work among the fishing fleet.

"They are not only given physical help in time of disaster, but they want to hold simple religious services and to oppose the work of the vessels that sell liquor to the fishermen. They want a doctor to go with the boat, one who will enter into the spiritual phase of the work, hoping that through the medical, interest may be enlisted in the spiritual."

Grenfell was thrilled by the opportunity, for it combined his interest in medicine, adventure and Christian humanitarianism. Gladly he accepted the offer and made preparations to leave. He went aboard the vessel at Yarmouth. Here he was taken aback at the smallness of the craft, not much larger than the ones in which he and his brother had sailed during those long and unforgettable summers.

On deck he found a capable and cordial skipper as well as a healthy and congenial crew. On the starboard bow were the words "Heal the sick," and on the port, "Jesus said, 'Follow me and I will make you fishers of men.'"

After a short trip to Ostend, Belgium, for a cargo which was to be sold to the fishermen at a price lower than that at which the commercial boats could sell it, the boat headed out into the open sea, where Dr. Grenfell was to serve two months on what proved to be the opening venture into a career which God was preparing for him. Out there, far beyond the shorelines, with only an occasional glimpse of land, the young doctor served the sick and wounded faithfully. Here he found more than twenty thousand men and boys, taking the difficult with the easy, a joyful and merry lot. Daily his admiration for the men grew, and he was eager to serve his Saviour by serving them.

Each fishing fleet, he discovered, was ruled by an admiral and vice-admiral, selected jointly by the fleet owner and skippers of the boats. Operations were flag-directed during the day, and at night were guided by rockets. Grenfell, in the little mission boat, thrilled at the fleet of sailing boats scudding before the wind, like white-winged birds during the day, and at night dotting the waves with lights and rockets blinking and arcing the sky. The mission boat sailed among those in the fleet, and the doctor helped the men, as opportunity offered or demanded, both physically and morally.

An outcome of the mission work was the Fisher Lad's Letter Writing Association, in which members pledged themselves to write regularly to orphan boys at sea, and, if possible, to care for them whenever they went ashore.

When the fishing days ended, the young doctor, thoroughly interested in and devoted to such ventures, became, during the summer vacation, medical officer in a camp for public-school boys. The venture was new, and the camps were located on land lent by an owner, property which was usually located near the sea. Grenfell fell in happily with the idea, which had sprouted in the fertile brains of Cambridge and Oxford men. The instruction was military in character, but it included games, gymnastics, bathing, hiking, boating and other athletics, with prominent athletes taking part in the program to deepen the boy's enthusiasm. Each evening a capable speaker gave a talk on morals, freely discussing boys' problems. Many a lad, Grenfell was to learn in later years, reached the turning point in his life during these camp sessions.

But the doctor's first love was his work among the fisher folk which continued to develop as public interest increased and other vessels were added to the first service boat. Queen Victoria expressed her approbation and purchased for the fleet a hospital boat which was graciously named in her honor. Grenfell watched as a shore institute for fishermen was opened at Yarmouth, and a dispensary vessel was sent in the spring to work among the Scotch, Irish, Manx and French fishermen off the south and west coasts of Ireland.

Here the doctor sailed the rugged coast, answering calls for medical help from fishermen and the on-shore poor as well. A social center and dispensary was established at Crookhaven, to be followed by a second at Kerry Coast. On Sundays, services were held on the boats and song-fests were conducted wherever the men could be gathered. Loving music, hymns and addresses, the men were cheered as these forces touched their hard, and many times unhappy, lives.

Thus until 1891, when he was called suddenly to London, Dr. Grenfell, then twenty-six, served the fishing fleets in an effort to bring the men physical comfort and the spiritual healing of the Gospel. On this London visit, Francis Hopwood, later Lord Southborough, met Grenfell and, as a member of the Mission Board, told him of his recent visit to Canada and Newfoundland, and that he had spoken to the Board's council. He also told of the need of Atlantic coast fishermen. When the discussion ended, Grenfell was asked, "Would you consider crossing the Atlantic in one of the Mission's small sailing vessels and looking into the project?"

The doctor's love for adventure, the thought of sailing those iceland shores, of working among hardier and even braver fishermen than those of the North Sea, conditioned him to accept God's call to service. God and Grenfell joined in a humanity-serving venture which was to bring to the lonely huts along the frozen shores of Labrador the comfort of the Gospel and relief for their physical hardships.

# Chapter 3

# *THE LURE OF LABRADOR*

GOD SET THE SAILS of Wilfred Grenfell's life toward Labrador. His entire career until this time had been a preparation for the great field of service where he was to serve and glorify the Master. He was not to be only a doctor sailing a mercy ship among the North Sea fishermen. God was to place him in a sphere of labor where he could perform year-round service, bringing hope and the Gospel to men for whom little had been done.

The call was clear, and throughout the winter of 1891-1892 Grenfell was busy making preparations for the coming voyage across the Atlantic. He was to be a modern Columbus, discovering a new land and bringing to light the problems and privations of a group of people long lost to the world.

On inspecting the mercy ship, he found it unsuited for the task at hand, and he spent the entire winter making it shipshape as a sailing hospital. The Mission Board furnished a ketch-rigged boat, much like a yawl, which was to sail in waters infested with floes and icebergs. Grenfell immediately installed nursing bunks, built an operating table and set up a dispensary. The hatches, small, so

31

that they might keep out the wind-driven waters, had to be enlarged so that patients could be carried below.

The boat, not much larger than the *Matthew*, in which John Cabot had discovered Newfoundland in 1497, was named the *Albert*, and during the second week of June, 1892, the vessel turned its prow westward with flags flying and friends from the dock waving a spirited farewell. Grenfell's plan was to make a nonstop trip, but so wild were the winds and foggy the weather that the skipper, Captain Trevize, put to shore at Crookhaven, where the Mission had previously built a dispensary and social center. Here the voyagers were given a glorious welcome and the vessel was piled high with fresh eggs and "greens" for the outbound trip.

During seventeen fog-bound days the *Albert* plowed through the wave-wracked Atlantic, when suddenly the fog banks disappeared, the sun shone clear, and there far ahead stood a high coastline crowned with evergreen trees. Grenfell saw a lighthouse on a rocky headlands, and knew at once that the *Albert* had nosed itself like an arrow to its target into St. John's Harbor, the Newfoundland port to which the skipper directed his course.

The doctor saw that billows of smoke were rising over the city, and as the pilot tug took the Albert in tow they were told that St. John's was in flames and virtually destroyed. Despite this the people courageously welcomed the mercy ship. The city's governor, the prime minister of Newfoundland and other officials were on hand to join in the rites of welcome. Grenfell, who had expected to work among the fishing schooners on the Big Banks as he had with the North Sea fleets, was told that this was impractical because of the heavy fogs which separated the boats.

It was suggested that the wiser plan was to follow the large fleet that had just sailed north for summer work along the Labradorian coast. The doctor learned, on inquiry, that a hundred vessels carrying nearly thirty thousand fishermen and their wives and children, made up the fleet. Accepting the advice, the skipper gladly welcomed a government-furnished pilot, and Adolph Nielson, superintendent of fisheries, offered to accompany the doctor on the voyage, and gave expert knowledge and advice concerning fish and the men who lived by them. Northward the *Albert* ploughed for another four hundred miles, sailing first along the Newfoundland coast and then cutting across the Bell Isle Straits to the Labradorian shoreline.

On August 4, 1892, Grenfell thrilled at the glorious sight of Labrador. Before him stretched the land to which God had directed him. His heart leaped at the challenge. Writing twenty-five years after the event, and speaking often of it, he describes the memory of that day, "which will die only when I do." The glorious sun burst over the oily blue of the ocean. Grenfell counted more than a hundred icebergs that lifted their gleaming heads above the waves. All the colors of the rainbow flashed from their gleaming pinnacles.

Birds both familiar and strange swung skyward in long arcs as they raced up from the schools of rippling fish. The large islands, verdure-crowned, its peaks shawled in the icy mists of early morning, "rose in a setting of the purest azure blue." Though forty years had passed, still the magnificent vision did not fade from Grenfell's memory. He looked upon Labrador, kissed by white breakers from the gigantic swells that hurled mountains of water upon its bastions, and he listened to the thunder of the ocean, like the sound of mighty drums beaten by giants in some far-off place. Looking, he thrilled at the thought of the challenge he faced.

Everywhere he could see schools of whales, slapping the surface of the sea with their boisterous tails, diving out of the water like frolicsome overgrown children. Shoals of fish which stirred beneath the *Albert* gave proof to the statement that "the whole vast ocean was too small to hold its riches."

Newfoundland companions whispered the story of the land's past and present into the doctor's ears as the ship ploughed northward. He had studied the maps enough to know that the island lay in the same latitude as England, and Battle Harbor, where later much of his work was to center, is almost directly in line with London. Grenfell remembered the Gulf Stream which lapped the Irish Sea, warming his homeland, as he felt the icy blast of the currents that swept down from the North Pole and froze the Labradorian coast. Biting winds and dripping mists swept in as he recalled the tales of brave John Cabot, discoverer of New Found Land (as he called it).

On the second voyage, 1498, so Grenfell was informed by his sailing companions, the adventurer had come upon the icy finger which was Labrador, named by Corte Real, in 1501, *Terra Labrador*, meaning "Workable Land," in contradistinction to *Terra Verde*, or "Green Land."

Sailing northward to join the fleet, he could not destroy the vision of the jutting peninsula which is Labrador. One historian, so the doctor was informed, had declared, "God made the world in five days, made Labrador on the sixth, and spent the seventh throwing stones at it." Said another, "There is nothing in it of any value." But Grenfell, filled with God-given compassion, saw jewels to be polished for his King.

The sensitive doctor found it a beautiful land rising to the height of two or three thousand feet, and blessed with innumerable islands that dotted the sea. The deep-cut fjords winding their way inland lured one to explore them. He watched as the waterfalls leaped down the mountain walls to race seaward as torrential rivulets.

As the story of this strange land poured into Grenfell's heart, he had many thoughts. Here were fish, boundless oceans of wealth swimming in the waters, and on land were wild fur-bearing animals which when the waters froze and drove the fisherfolk to land, could be trapped in their lairs on the bays and fjords. In the summer, he discovered, numerous people lived here—Americans brushed shoulders with the Canadians, who in turn jostled the British, competed with the Newfoundlanders, fought with the Indians and outwitted the Eskimos.

Strange were the stories told Grenfell about the superstitions and customs of this land. The head of a fox or wolf, hung from the ceiling, for instance, was supposed to show the windrift. Nails cut on Monday prevented boils, and the haddock's fin bone was thought to charm away rheumatic ills.

On they sailed, and Grenfell continued to learn about the strange land to which his heart was being drawn. Said one, "A summer population of fishermen and their families of nearly thirty thousand." Declared another, "Dwindling to less than four thousand when the bitter winter winds blizard-sweep the land." "And they fish in the summer, and the winters are given to trapping," said another, to be supported by the statement, "Around seventeen hundred Eskimos live here."

Coming to a channel that raced between two cliffs, the pilot said, "That is Domino Run. The boats all pass through here on their way to and from the fishing grounds."

Here the doctor found an excellent harbor, and the *Albert* sailed in, dropped anchor and raised aloft its flag which bore the inscription *Mission to Deep Sea Fishermen*. Immediately flags fluttered their greetings from vessels roundabout. The scene, lively and beautiful, stirred the doctor's imagination. The fishing boats, riding the swells, rose and dipped joyously, and the bunting danced in the breeze.

Soon the boats raced to draw alongside the mercy ship, and when they were told that a doctor was on board, and the ship, a veritable floating hospital, was to spend the summer with the fleet, a glad acclaim arose from the vessels. Soon patients began to arrive in a steady stream until evening dwindled them out. As the rays of the lowering sun slanted far out into the ocean, Grenfell noticed a small and dilapidated boat, the *Darby*, draw alongside. In it sat a wizened man.

"Be you a real doctor?" he asked, hesitatingly as though the hope was too wonderful to be real.

When Grenfell assured the stranger that he was a doctor, the news almost stunned the fisherman.

"Us hasn't any money," he continued, "but there's a sick man ashore, if so be you'd come and see him."

The doctor climbed into the rickety craft and was taken to shore, where, on landing, he followed the man to a hovel which was more miserable than the most poverty-stricken hut he had ever seen. It had one window of patched glass. The floor was made of pebbles, and the dank bunk-lined walls dripped moisture. Huddled in the corner were six disheveled children. In a bunk lay a sick man wracked by a hammerlike cough, as a thinly-clad woman dripped cold water into his mouth with a spoon.

Thought the doctor, *Little can be done for him in these surroundings . . . pneumonia . . . raging fever . . . symptoms of tuberculosis.*

The kindly physician did what he could for the patient, but pronounced his case as near-hopeless under the prevailing circumstances. He thought, *Here, in the new field, are needs beyond those of the fishing fleet itself.*

For two months the *Albert* journeyed along the coast and among the fleet, where the doctor studied the work and its possibilities and treated the sick and injured as they came to him. During this time nine hundred cases came under his care, some of which lingered long in his memory. One was an Eskimo, who, when firing a cannon salute in honor of the arrival of a Moravian Mission ship, had blown off both arms below the elbow. No medical help had been at hand, and the man had lain for some time with the stumps, bloody and gangrenous, covered with dirty rags which were dipped occasionally into cold water. Grenfell found a sixteen-year-old lad dying of hip disease in an incredibly dirty hovel. Everything was covered with vermin, and for months the lad had lain thus.

Dr. Grenfell discovered that lack of dental care also caused intense suffering. One boy he especially remembered whose face had been drawn out of shape because of an infected bone resulting from a bad tooth. He found also the deformed, the maimed, the blind, the tubercular, those suffering from rickets and even those dying from contagious diseases.

As Grenfell traveled, the desperate call for social work, as well as medical care, education and sanitation, challenged him. Ever practical, Grenfell realized that the introduction of better modes of living would be a blessing to the forsaken people. In one village where he stopped, a woman with seven children asked to be married to her husband, their father. She explained that whenever anyone had come to the village who could marry them, her husband was away. Fortunately a minister was on board the ship, and the wedding was duly celebrated. The villagers attended and the ship bells rang jubilantly as the guns were fired.

The doctor, also a humanitarian and naturalist, was thrilled by the natural beauty around him. Everywhere fjords lured him as they wound through the high cliffs and fairly shouted their invitations to guide his boat in and out on explorations. Evergreen trees shone in the sunshine. The streams made him long to drop his hook for the trout and salmon. Islands beckoned him, and applying his hydrographic skill, he mapped them for future sailings.

Overhead he saw strange birds as they soared in the
blue, and underfoot he found unusual plants that stirred
his botanical interest. Geology, too, held him spellbound
as he saw the twisted rocks and raised beaches. Stone
arrows and stone knives, given him by friendly Eskimos
and fisher folk, spoke of the Vikings of long-ago days.
Day by day he found new challenges to his attention,
and he collected many items for the museum which he
hoped someday to have.

Finally the day arrived when Grenfell watched the pilot
as he whirled the *Albert* about with the wind and sailed
southward. One morning when he came on board, he found
ice crystals sparkling along the boat's waterline, and he
knew it would be tragic for the ship to be clutched in the
frozen maw of an ice pack. Returning to Domino Run,
he could not resist the opportunity to visit the first case
he had attended in Labrador, and was heartbroken to find
that the man had died.

He thought, *If only there had been a hospital, the man
need not have died!*

The widow, he was informed, would receive a miserable
grant of twenty dollars a year to be spent for food. This
presented another problem which Dr. Grenfell could not
dismiss, and as he pondered the past two months work,
he found many types of service calling, needs which he felt
demanded the attention of Gospel workers. They needed
education, which demanded schools. The children must be
cared for, which created the demand for a bureau of organized child welfare. Industrial and economic problems
cried for solution, no less than the acute medical and
dental needs.

*How can these calls be met?* he asked himself, as the
*Albert* sailed to St. John's.

On arriving he found that news of his work had sped
ahead of him and prepared a welcome homecoming. Returning fishermen had told of the help he had given,

and praised his Samaritan acts so enthusiastically that the Board of Trade commended his services. Newspapers publicized the stories, and the governor called a meeting at which a resolution was passed commending Grenfell's excellent work among the Labradorian needy as well as with the fishing fleets.

The group thanked the Deep Sea Mission and its directors for the mercy ship *Albert* which had visited the settlements on the Labradorian coast: ". . . much of our fishing industry is carried on in regions beyond the ordinary reach of medical aid, or of charity, and it is with the deep sense of gratitude that this meeting learns of the amount of medical and surgical work done."

The governor's meeting added the wish and prayer that "the directors may see their way to continue the work thus begun, and should they do so, they may be assured of the earnest co-operation of all classes of this community."

There were more tangible expressions of gratitude which the doctor found waiting him. The most successful mercantile company of the colony, the Baine, Johnston and Company, had startled the governor's group by promising to provide a building for the work at Battle Harbor. With this happy news to carry with him, the doctor watched gladly as the *Albert* sailed out of the harbor for the home port.

On reaching the Mission's London headquarters he told the news that a building had been given for the project in Labrador, and the Board thanked the Heavenly Father for His benediction upon the work which had been undertaken in faith and dependence upon Him. As Grenfell and the skipper, Captain Trevize, traveled about England addressing meetings and telling about the plight of the Labradorians, their story aroused interest, and money began to come in to outfit a second and more extensive trip.

Funds in the Mission treasury permitted the purchase of better equipment, and soon the Board was again thrilled by the news that the Job Brothers, a Newfoundland firm with fisheries at Indian Harbor, some two hundred miles north of Battle Harbor, had offered to erect a hospital at the site of their fisheries. Thus there were to be two hospitals to be staffed with doctors and nurses.

These blessings raised a new and vexing problem, that of transportation between the two places. While meditating on the problem and seeking a solution, Dr. Grenfell learned that a small steam launch, forty-five feet long and eight wide, riding at anchor on the Dee near his old Parkgate home was for sale at the ridiculously low price of forty-five dollars. Immediately a friend furnished the money and Wilfred's brother rejuvenated the vessel. At an appropriate ceremony the doctor christened the ship the *Princess May,* and it was swung aboard an ocean liner for the trans-Atlantic trip.

Nor was the call for medical assistance unanswered, for soon two young doctors and two trained nurses volunteered for the service, which meant a doctor and nurse for each hospital, while Dr. Grenfell remained free for coast-cruising in the *Princess May.* This would enable him to reach the hospitals. Thus with a bright outlook, more glorious than that of the previous year, the *Albert* once more pushed westward.

God had opened the door, prepared the man, provided circumstances in England and Labrador, and now Grenfell was ready to go wherever the Divine Hand would lead. God had answered the doctor's prayers for a sphere where he could profitably invest his life, and now, sailing once more on the familiar *Albert,* which was to take him on the grandest adventure any Grenfell had ever had, Wilfred was being true to the tradition of his ancestors.

Deeply conscious of God's blessings hitherto and the divine purpose running like a golden thread throughout his entire life, he gave himself seriously to prayer that the new venture might be thoroughly successful. He saw, in imagination, islands of human desolation and need which he must conquer for Christ and to which he must bring social as well as spiritual benefits. The dream lured him on, and eagerly he laid the groundwork for his future career. "Christ First" became his slogan. He knew that God would supply the "all these things"—and He did.

# Chapter 4

## SAILING UNKNOWN WATERS

GOD HAD MIRACULOUSLY answered prayer that Labrador's doors might be thrown open to medical and Gospel work. Little had the brave doctor dreamed that two hospitals would be erected in this chosen land which the Almighty had laid so heavily upon his heart, and as he sailed west- ward through the chilly Atlantic waters, he dreamed of the vast opportunities for Christian service. First of all he was a doctor, trained to care for the sick, but, above all, to express his Christianity in a practical manner.

Medicine and Christianity were handmaidens, each sup- plementing the other. The doctor was also a Gospel worker: he healed the body that this physical benefit might promote spiritual healing. In Labrador there were many calls for such service. As Grenfell began his career, somewhat new in the annals of missionary work (most missionaries had first been preachers and then doctors) he was to blaze a trail for others to follow.

Arriving at St. John's, he and his medical assistants were overjoyed to discover that already the Battle Harbor hospital was half completed, and soon the nurses would walk among its sixteen beds, eight for men and a similar number for women. Grenfell assigned Dr. Bobardt and one of the nurses to this hospital as their place of practical Christian service.

On inquiry he found that the Indian Harbor hospital would not be ready for occupancy until the following year. With two boats to be manned, Dr. Grenfell turned the *Albert* over to Dr. Curwen, the other of the two volunteer physicians, with instructions that he was to sail the Labradorian waters in search of patients who needed hospitalization. This implied following the fleet of fishermen as well as sailing along the shore and visiting the settlements where sick might be found.

Grenfell reserved the small *Princess May,* a valiant little steam launch, for himself that he might sail in and out of the coastal islands, chart new regions, and visit the sick who did not require hospital aid. The problems presented by such were numerous indeed and called for unusual skill and almost uncanny sailing ability.

First Dr. Grenfell must familiarize himself with the coast, chart its islands, explore its shoals, sail into its creeks, outline its harbors, skirt the headlands and study tides and ocean currents, which demanded the skill of a sailor and the practical knowledge of an experienced captain and explorer. This challenged the adventuresome spirit of the doctor, who as a lad had dreamed of such days.

Northward there was no lighthouse, which demanded careful sailing, nor had there been done much accurate charting of the coastline. The fogs were thick, blotting out, as the doctor was to find by experience, the shoals, islands, headlands, bays and, at times, even the vessels. Grenfell felt himself appointed to do this explorative work as well as to heal the sick and bring Christ to the needy.

For this great task the slim *Princess May* seemed a frail craft, but as she steamed out of St. John's harbor on July 7, 1893, the twenty-eight-year-old skipper on board was stout of heart and ready for any adversity. His crew

consisted of a cook and an engineer, neither of whom
had any more practical knowledge of the coast than he
himself.

"Two bits of ice will crack her like a nutshell," pre-
dicted some, to be seconded by others, who laughed, "An
iceberg will wipe her out like a man stepping on a flea."

Still others forecast dismally, "She'll be swamped by the
swells and the wind."

Nor were these predictions long coming dangerously
near fulfillment, for soon she began shipping water, and as
the doctor watched the water creep higher and higher, he
made a hasty survey of the vessel and soon discovered
a nasty leak and plugged it hastily.

Leaky seams were not the only threat to their safety.
They had barely caulked the hole when a dense fog slipped
sinisterly over the *Princess May,* and when the fog lifted
they were confronted by an angry cliff.

With a tug the doctor swung the wheel, with more speed
than had ever swung at the ball on a cricket field, and
he watched as they barely escaped being crushed on the
shore. Wondering why they had swerved from their set
course, Dr. Grenfell found that the compass zigzagged an
uneven course rather than pointing to earth's magnetic
pole. Correcting this deflection from the true course,
slowly, as the fog held, they crept onward, inching by
degrees through the surf, among the rocks and over the
shoals. The reefs were many and the pilot-doctor cautiously
worked farther out into the deeper waters.

Before night settled they steamed into a small harbor,
where they found shelter, and thus the first sailing day
passed, as many thousands were to stretch in an almost
endless procession during the next forty-five years.

Thus he edged his way northward, working slowly up
the coast about two-thirds of the length of the peninsula,
and went as far as Okkak. He dropped into small out-of-
the-way settlements and steamed into tiny inlets and creeks

where a larger vessel could not be navigated. When possible, arrangements were made for the patients to be taken to the Battle Harbor hospital, thus saving much suffering and many patients' lives.

He found in these various places people, men, women and children who for years had patiently suffered, enduring agony so intense that death would have furnished welcome release. A short visit to the hospital sometimes enabled them to return home strong and able to take up their accustomed work.

During the summer Dr. Grenfell worked his way toward the Arctic, familiarizing himself with the coast and preparing the pattern for his future voyages. He was urged onward that he might meet the Moravian missionaries on their home grounds where they labored with the Eskimos. He was to find that in the previous hundred and thirty years these brave folk had been able to build five stations, which in summer dotted the northward shorelines and in winter were buried deep in snow.

Since there had been no recent charting of this watery section, little explorative work having been done since the days of Captain Cook, one of the Moravian brethren accompanied the *Princess May* on this journey in order that Grenfell might find the northern stations and cut a way through the plethora of islands which fringed the coastline.

Traveling through an endless chain of fjords, steaming into bays and straights, often they did not see the open sea for days. "Never in my life," the doctor affirms in telling of those marvelous experiences, "had I expected any journey half so wonderful." The little steamer threaded a path between high mountains and sailed under the lee of towering cliffs. Often they crossed the mouths of large rivers, seeing on either side groves of spruce, fir and larches as they lined the banks.

Overhead flocked convoys of Canadian geese, eider ducks and more common seafowl. Since sailing was possible only in daylight, before night darkened the shore, Grenfell and his men would enter some tiny bay or inlet where they tied up and spent their time gathering specimens of abundant and beautiful subarctic plants and foods. Occasionally they captured a bird or caught a mess of trout for the evening meal.

Since the Moravians worked principally with the Eskimos and had no doctors among their station staffs, the skipper, whose hands were as familiar with the wheel as with the scalpel, found all that he could do in treating the patients who lined the missionary buildings along the way. Frame houses had long since taken the place of skin tents, homes for the Eskimos during the summer, and ice huts, which had provided shelter in winter. These frame homes, so the missionaries affirmed, were more sanitary, but as the doctor saw the garbage which littered their floors he found little sanitation of any kind.

The dirty huts were filth-covered, nor did they have provisions for sanitation and lacked any type of water supply. Hence health conditions were appalling, and tuberculosis and eye diseases were rampant.

The doctor enjoyed his visits with the Eskimos, who were good natured, loved music immensely—they even had a band of their own!—and laughed often. They seemed content with their lot in life and as they sang, their dirty faces glowed with joy. When Grenfell made records of their songs and replayed them, the natives were delighted as their "canned" voices left the machine. On a second trip to one of the stations, he showed some slides he had previously made of them, and when he showed a picture of a woman who had since died, the people made a great commotion, thinking that her spirit had returned to haunt them.

The trip was valuable in that it showed the doctor the evil of any missionary system which became a trading mission. Here among the Moravians he found the trading

system to be in vogue, and this kept the Eskimos con-
tinually in debt to the mission. The plan was common
in Labrador and it created much hardship, for it fostered
the debt habit and kept the people always in bondage to
the trader or mission store. Furthermore, this system
made it possible for the mission or other trader to set any
price on the native goods, or his own merchandise, that
he chose, and thus the Eskimo was frequently cheated. This
also took away the native's freedom to sell to the highest
bidder. Later, when Grenfell was working out the economic
and industrial structure of the Labradorian mission, he
sought to remedy this condition.

In his tours he discovered that the Moravians had opened
a school for the Eskimos at Nain, and at another point,
Makkovik, they maintained a boarding school for the
natives, where the more intelligent were sent for training.
Years later, inspired by Dr. Grenfell's Labradorian hospitals, they also opened a hospital at Okkak, which cared for
the natives' physical needs as the mission stations long
had provided for their spiritual welfare.

The dangers of ice always threatened the pilot's ships,
and as summer came to a close, the doctor found it necessary to steam speedily to St. John's port, lest the *Princess
May* be frozen in for the winter and crushed like an egg-
shell by the powerful ice. As the little launch steamed
southward, the explorer-missionary retraced his steps, and
usually as he stopped at the settlements visited earlier, Dr.
Grenfell held simple services, showed lantern slides, dis-
pensed pills where needed, diagnosed serious cases and,
if possible, performed minor surgical operations.

With the rapid development of the Labradorian work,
Grenfell was convinced that the Mission to Deep Sea Fishermen in England ought to be partially, at least, if not totally,
relieved of the responsibility of supporting the project.
Desiring to seek financial aid from other sources, he turned
his attention toward Southern Newfoundland and Canada,

*Wilfred Grenfell*

where he planned a lecture tour with slides of what was being undertaken. His first lecture was given in St. John's, from which he went to neighboring towns, such as Grace Harbor and Carbonear.

Since these places were small, he discovered that the sectarian spirit ran high, so he and Dr. Bobardt, formerly in charge of the Battle Harbor hospital and who was now accompanying Grenfell on the lecture tour, decided that they would cross to Halifax in Nova Scotia, where they hoped to carry their campaign for funds farther afield.

The work was new to both, and their personal expense money was about to "run aground." At their first breakfast enjoyed in Canada they discussed the situation and reached the conclusion that they should lift the white flag of surrender. Carrying letters of introduction from leading men of Newfoundland, they did not know how to proceed with their venture. Though the sea had long been home to the doctor, he found himself in an expanseless sea of perplexities with no place of anchorage.

Bobardt came forward with the suggestion, when Grenfell's spirits had shipped too much water to remain afloat much longer, that they call personally upon the leading people of the town—the prime minister, ranking military officials, the president of the Board of Trade, the governor of the province and even the leading clergymen. While Grenfell thought this a bit presumptuous, he was able to think of no better scheme, and willingly accompanied the other doctor on the round of visits.

Everywhere the two men were gladly received, and when they told of their mission work along the Labradorian coast the people listened with excitement at the bravery displayed in the venture of faith. Committees were formed to support two beds in the hospital and to contribute supplies, and when they had finished their task, armed with letters of introductions and endorsements they set out for

Montreal, where they hoped to continue their fund-raising campaign.

Reaching Montreal, their own finances were in a deplorable state. The younger doctor suggested that they register at the finest hotel in the city, which to Grenfell seemed a bit bold, but when Bobardt at length had his way, he registered as an Australian, since he was a native of that far-flung outpost of the Empire. This led to long interviews with reporters and pieces in the papers about a better understanding between Canada and Australia in trade relations.

His psychology proved right, for at once the mission was given sympathetic understanding and attention. Lord Strathcona, president of the Hudson Bay Company, the Canadian Pacific Railroad and the Bank of Montreal, became deeply interested in the work, and this interest continued throughout his life. As Donald Smith, a poor Scotch lad, he had lived thirteen years in Labrador, and there had met his wife. His first daughter also had been born in that land.

He willingly consented to be chairman of the first meeting, which gave the lecture a favorable introduction to the people of the city. Dr. Bobardt (to save expenses) decided to act as ticket seller. Not having met the lord previously, when he presented himself at the door, Bobardt insisted that he pay the usual fifty-cent admission fee. Sir Donald protested, saying that he was to preside at the meeting as chairman. Calmly the doctor said, "Three others have told me the same thing, and I demand that you pay the fee."

Sir Donald presented his money for admission, and the doctor's businesslike attitude pleased him greatly, binding his heart more closely to the project. So great was his love for the work that he gave the mission an excellent, though small, steamer for coastal travel. On discovering that neither Grenfell nor Bobardt had seen Canada, he arranged an expense-free trip that they might visit the nation

as far west as British Columbia. He even made it possible
for them to ride in the engine through the beautiful Canadian wilds and the western mountains. On the trip Grenfell
was greatly interested to see many thousands of miles of
excellent farming land with few if any residents.

On finishing the journey and completing their lecture
tour, the two doctors sailed for England, well satisfied
with the results of this faith venture. Dr. Bobardt entered
the British Navy, but when summer came, Grenfell again
felt the pull of Labrador, to which he had given his heart,
so he sailed once more for St. John's. He brought back
with him more volunteer workers. Loading the *Albert* with
more supplies than he had previously taken, he sent it on
to Battle Harbor, while he himself went to Montreal to receive Lord Strathcona's wonderful gift, the boat.

Steaming out of Montreal with the vessel, en route to
Battle Harbor, he visited friends, spoke about his work
where occasion presented, and enjoyed the delightful voyage. When he had almost reached the hospital, resplendent
with flying flags, polished brass, and gleaming white paint,
an expectant crowd had already gathered at the harbor
to welcome them, when suddenly the *Sir Donald* crashed
on a submerged rock and toppled over.

Quickly Grenfell's one-man crew investigated the damage
done by the wreck, only to bear the sad news that the
side was ripped, the propeller and shaft torn out and the
keel splintered. Almost in tears, the doctor stood aghast
as he surveyed the wreckage. There was nothing to be
done but row with his fellow crewmen to the nearest island,
where he finally found a fisherman to take him and the
crew to Battle Harbor. Here, bedraggled and crestfallen,
they told the sad news to their impatient friends.

Helpers rushed to the rescue, and equipped with tools,
they crowded into boats and soon had the *Sir Donald* repaired sufficiently to be towed the three hundred miles or
more to St. John's. This delay meant that the ship would

be idle for the summer, and the noble humanitarian work planned for her had to be entrusted to another.

Fortunately, however, Sir Thomas Roddick, also of Montreal, but a native son of Newfoundland, had given the mission a smaller boat, shipping some twenty-feet of water, with a sail and center boom, which was to give Dr. Grenfell further experience in sailing Labradorian waters despite difficulties and handicaps. With this vessel he carried on his summer work, cruising along the coast at a much lower rate of speed but doing his work efficiently nevertheless. What he lacked in equipment he made up in determination not to be deterred in carrying out God's plan.

Too small to ship sufficient supplies for the summer, the boat served a higher purpose than the doctor knew, and this supposed handicap became a blessing in disguise, for he was forced to go to the settlements more often for supplies and to live "off the country." This brought him into intimate contact with the villagers and caused the people whom he was serving to be drawn closer to their benefactor. He found them to be a hospitable folk, helpful in time of need and characterized by a lightheartedness not often found even among those whose blessings are greater.

It was at this time that he built a sincere love between himself and the people, and they were knit together in the undertaking to which Dr. Grenfell had devoted his life.

That summer Grenfell went as far north in the little boat as Eskimo Bay, picking his way between the islands, and using a local pilot when available. The homeward journey was marked by near-tragedy in the form of a storm which threatened to produce dire results. Coming to Square Island Harbor, a settlement of a dozen or so families, later than he had planned in sailing southward, the boat became storm-bound in the harbor and on inquiry the doctor found that the season's catch had been insignificant indeed, all too small to run the group through the coming eight months of bad weather, and to add to the calamity the trading vessels going south for the winter had passed the harbor.

This presaged semistarvation, if not death. On meeting the people, Dr. Grenfell came to the village patriarch, belovedly called "Uncle Jim," who invited the honored guest from the south to stay at his house. The doctor, accepting events as they came and believing them to be from a wise and loving God, did not worry about the predicament in which he found himself. The villagers, on the contrary, were frantic with fear. Only Uncle Jim, a man of faith and prayer, was steadfast in his confidence that relief was on the way.

Uncle Jim prayed diligently for deliverance from the storm's clutches, and as he prayed, he remembered the promise of God. Dr. Grenfell's faith likewise grew stronger. The people were called to a prayer meeting at Uncle Jim's, and together they poured out their hearts for themselves and their children, hungry and destitute. There was little the doctor could do to help the group, except to express his belief that deliverance was near. Uncle Jim, too, did not waver in his assurance that help was on the way.

Bright and early the next morning when Dr. Grenfell looked out upon the harbor, there rode a trader's vessel at anchor, which had been driven there by the raging storm and had already passed the villagers. The people, their prayers answered gloriously, received their supplies, and lives were saved also. The storm's fury having blown out, Dr. Grenfell sailed away, thankful that he could be a living witness to the truth that God rules and leads.

When another summer came, the doctor was eager to be back at his cruising and exploring once more, for by now the *Sir Donald* had been repaired and was ready for whatever course the skipper would select. This time the doctor guided the mercy vessel, laden with food and medical supplies, far northward to the uppermost tip of eastern Labrador to Cape Chidley. On this journey into the little-known region he discovered that Cape Chidley was really on an island, and not on the mainland.

He explained this northward course by saying that the fishing schooners had gone into these uncharted northern waters during the summer and he was thus able to treat a number of their sick and injured. For instance, on a schooner near Ungava Bay, he saw the flag at half mast, a signal for aid, and going aboard, he discovered a young fisherman writhing in agony from a gun wound that had ruptured his eye.

The doctor dressed the eye cautiously and relieved the pain so that the lad could return to his work, but Grenfell was fearful of the outcome. The boy became apprehensive as he wondered what his girl friend would think when he returned in the fall. The doctor recalled that a pair of glass eyes had been included in the equipment for the Battle Harbor hospital, so he told the lad to stop there on his homeward journey and have one fitted, thus removing the fear of his friend's reaction when she discovered that he had lost an eye.

Later that fall, Grenfell was asked by a young man to look at one of his eyes. The doctor could not stop just then but asked the young fellow to come to the hospital, where he would examine the eye later.

"I'm the boy whose eye you took out, and you told me to come here for a glass one," laughed the young man. "Do you think it will suit her?"

He encountered all types of cases as he sailed among the islands and with the fishing fleet. This time he had remained northward, and at Battle Harbor, longer than he should have. Consequently, when trips ashore were necessary to visit the sick, he had to use dog teams, as the ground was covered with snow. Finally he worked his way down to Henley, where his party was fogbound and almost shipwrecked. But through the skipper's quick action, the catastrophe was averted.

The work of Grenfell and his associates had changed the people's attitude toward professional medical help. Gradually modern miracles of healing were being performed. The blind were made to see, and often the lame walked from the hospital. Many whom the folk termed "incurables" had been healed, and faith in charms, amulets, haddock fins and praying scrolls began to waver.

In fact, the preference for skilled help was so decided that a series of pleas went forth for the hospital to be kept open all winter. At first Dr. Grenfell did not think this feasible as the Battle Harbor building was not winterproofed, but when Dr. Willway volunteered to remain, provided Grenfell thought such a course wise, the physician decided to try the experiment.

All possible supplies on hand and equipment not absolutely needy on the homeward journey were left with the hospital doctor, and Grenfell and his associates sailed for England. They feared the results, especially since neither the remaining doctor nor the building were equipped for the long Arctic winter. Returning the following spring, to Grenfell's immense relief, Dr. Willway, hale and hearty despite the grueling months greeted the party. When he told Dr. Grenfell that during the winter he had dog-sledded eighteen hundred miles and treated many sick and injured, the physician could scarcely believe his ears.

One near-disaster, the doctor told them, had occurred. In relating the story, Willway said that the *Sir Donald* had been anchored in the harbor, and daily he looked out to see how it fared. One morning on looking out, even though the water was frozen solid, he was amazed to discover that the *Sir Donald* had simply disappeared without even leaving a mark in the ice where it had slipped either under or into the Atlantic. Nor could any sign of the wreckage be found.

Said the doctor, "It was evidently tired of harbor idleness, and longing for freedom in the open sea, she started out on a journey of her own, skipperless and without fire in her boilers."

They dragged the harbor for the craft, but she was not to be found. Then a down-the-coast search was begun, for someone surmised that the entire harbor ice floe had drifted to the open sea, taking the *Sir Donald* with it. Far away, sure enough, the boat was discovered, damaged not in the least. She was brought back to the harbor, but it was thought wise to sell the craft and raise funds for a ship better suited to the expanding work of the mission.

# Chapter 5

## WINTERING IN THE WILDS

FOR SOMETIME Dr. Grenfell, interestedly watching the seal industry, had considered trying to follow the seal hunters in their winter work, but since it was conducted during a difficult period of the season, he had not been permitted to do so. His interests were as broad as the lives of the people he was helping, and whatever interested them interested him.

He had heard how, when the warm spring sun began melting the frozen North, the seals rode down on the ice floes from the Arctic and a hundred miles east of Newfoundland. Temperature affected them little, since their thick silky fur coats kept them warm. About the middle of February they appeared in the Newfoundland waters, and within a week of their arrival, the baby seals were born. A month later the babies were plump little fellows weighing about fifty pounds each.

The government, Grenfell learned, prohibited killing seals before March 14 or after April 20. Likewise, the Newfoundland law prohibited taking the animals on Sundays. Hence the fishers must work fast, and the doctor knew that weeks before the hunt they gathered in St. John's, ready to dash to the seal grounds.

Dr. Grenfell's ears buzzed with stories Captain Samuel Blandford, senior skipper of the hunting fleet, had told him of hazards and the dire need for medical attention. Deciding to study these conditions first hand, Grenfell accepted the invitation of the *Neptune* to sail with him. The law forbade starting before two P.M. on March 10, and the doctor watched the schooners gather early in the harbor so that they might be ready to make the wild dash to the hunting floes. It was a gala occasion, and finally, when the hour struck, hundreds on shore cheered as the fleet leader, followed by the other boats, butted its way through the harbor.

The *Neptune* was a chubby bark-rigged vessel with auxiliary steam engines. The foot-and-a-half-thick hull was reinforced with tough green lumber as an added precaution against the ice. Ceiled with English oak, her bow was banded with iron, since stout vessels as well as iron-hearted men were needed for such labors. The crew of three hundred and twenty demanded supplies, and five hundred tons of coal were required by the engines that pushed the ship through the ice floes.

Sailing for days through floe-infested waters, the doctor looked out one morning and saw tiny black dots lining the ice fields in all directions. Instantly the men were over the *Neptune's* side, leaping from ice pan to ice pan. They were lightly dressed, so that they could race against time. Grenfell watched as they killed the animals, and hastily scalped and pelted them. Soon accident cases demanded his attention.

There were cuts to be bandaged, sprains to be taped, and snowblinded men to be given attention. The sport of seal-hunting appealed to the doctor's interest in athletics, and one day when his medical work was finished, he joined the men. Slipping over the ship's wet side, he raced to find the men, who were far out on the ice, and when he overtook them, it was midafternoon. The wintry winds, which had whipped the ocean all day, by this time had ceased, and hence the floes began to slip apart. Night came, and a handful of men who had managed to get together on the same floe decided to try to reach a near-by larger ice pan. But this proved impossible, and they were forced to remain in their present plight until the ship hove in sight.

The chilly winds whipped through their light clothes, and someone started to play leap frog. Others followed, and soon the men, led by the doctor, were hop-skip-and-jumping all over the little floe, leaping over each other's backs in a game they had played long ago. Using their wooden clubs with which they attacked the seals, they dipped them in seal fat and formed lighted torches to attract the *Neptune*. At long last the ship arrived, and when the doctor came on board the captain immediately gave him, as Grenfell calls it, "the worst blowing up I ever received since my father spanked me."

Apologizing for this later, the captain said he was so full of gratitude to God for delivering Grenfell from death that he did not know what he was saying.

On the last Sunday out, Dr. Grenfell held a religious service on board, a service he never forgot. The blazing sun bent down upon them, and the blue sky seemed to stretch boundlessly above the jostling mass of floes. Grenfell had brought along a number of small hymnals, and the men "lay out on the deck and sang and talked where they were unworried by callers and the thousand interruptions of the land." Then together they had evening prayers, Catholics and Protestants alike.

The sense of God's nearness and divine presence flooded Grenfell more gloriously, he affirms, than he had ever experienced it in the most magnificent cathedral. Eternal life seemed close by, "as if it lay just over the horizon of ice in the eternal blue beyond."

This trip impressed Grenfell with the economic waste of seal hunting. Since only one seal baby is born a year, and lives only a few weeks, Grenfell thought it disastrous that the animal should be murdered with no thought of the future supply of seals. On the other hand, the people living on those bleak shores viewed seal-hunting as their livelihood, and the government clambored for the revenue which came from the business. Consequently there was nothing Grenfell could do to check this waste in an industry which if rightly protected would prove a boon to thousands in the coming years.

A strange call came to Grenfell, and the answer demanded that he leave these Labradorian waters, much as he disliked doing so. His Mission asked him to go to Iceland with a view to opening work there, since the English fleets were traveling in those waters, and for the next three years, this work held his interest.

Returning to England, he sailed for Iceland, via Aberdeen, Scotland, where he visited the Seamen's Home. For some time the Mission had been fighting the liquor trade among the men and had been able to have it prohibited by international agreement, but as usual, bootleggers appeared, and the doctor wanted their business crushed. Grenfell, doing what he could for the temperance cause, journeyed to Iceland, and cruised around the island.

Here he saw a strange but happy people, living without many of civilization's benefits, and with few of its luxuries. He was amazed to find that the cows ate salt codfish and whales' tails, and the "goats grazed on the roofs of the houses," for here the only available grass was to be found.

On returning to the Mission Council with his recommendations, he said that the work would be difficult owing to the extensive fleet which fished the waters, and that only a steam hospital ship could answer the purpose. He likewise recommended a cottage hospital on land where the sick and injured could be taken.

Health conditions demanded that the doctor take a short vacation, and at the invitation of his former teacher,

Sir Frederick Treves, he spent some time at the doctor's home on the Scilly Islands, where, as a special favor, a regatta was held in the doctor's honor. Returning with renewed health, the following winter was spent in raising money for the Mission work and, in summer, visiting the North Sea fishing grounds, where he had first been inducted into what had become his life's career. When summer arrived once more, he sailed the waters around Ireland and inspected the activities which had been carried on by the Mission on and about the Emerald Isle.

During this time, Lord Strathcona had made a generous donation toward a boat to replace the *Sir Donald*. The new craft was to be a hospital ship, equipped with every modern appliance, built and equipped in England, and christened the *Strathcona*. English duties having been completed, Dr. Grenfell was happy when he could once more sail for Labrador, where the work, dear to his heart, was ably carried on by assistants. In October, 1899, he arrived at Battle Harbor, where salvos were fired from the guns and "flags gave us a welcome after three years' absence."

His heart was filled with gratitude to God for the mighty changes which had taken place since the day seven years earlier when he had first sailed into the harbor. He cried out, "What an oasis for patients from the bleak rocks outside!" At once he clamored for a ship with which to cruise the waters he loved. Since the *Strathcona* was not yet finished, he had to content himself with the small *Julia Sheridan*, a steam launch which a Toronto lady had provided to replace the *Sir Donald*.

Arriving in October, he had little time left for fall cruising, but when he felt the tingling air of Labrador against his cheeks, saw the gleaming ice and saw the northern lights playing in the sky, he was thrilled at the prospect of those wonderful days, even years, ahead in which he could serve his Master in what he now called the "home waters."

When the ice drove him from the open sea to winter quarters, he decided to investigate a call which had for some time been clamoring for attention. In England he had received many letters asking him to include northern Newfoundland in his missionary work and to establish a winter station at St. Anthony. One man whom he knew well had written: "Come and start a station here, if you can. My family is starving."

Another man with a large family told how for nine days they had subsisted without flour, living only on seal meat and calling for the doctor's aid. The truck system was in vogue in that section, which meant that the people traded or bartered their merchandise at whatever price the trader desired to place upon it in exchange for his goods.

The urge to investigate this call to St. Anthony was so strong that he took one of the assistants, Dr. Beattie, and went to the Newfoundland outpost, where he studied the prospects. They hired a couple of rooms in the principal trader's house, and engaged a guide, whom the doctor had previously used, as their dog driver. Since north and south of St. Anthony were smaller villages, they decided to visit these via dog sled.

The winter experience was one "long delight" to the doctor. He greatly enjoyed slipping over the ice hour after hour, viewing the snow-covered terrain, whose monotony was relieved by evergreen trees draped in a mantle of snow. This time he came into close contact with the people, and soon found that there were numerous opportunities to serve them.

Many were the calls for his help, and always he answered as God enabled him. On one occasion he visited a home at midnight, and found a boy with a broken hip. Thawing a frozen board for splints, he proceeded to pad the kitchen table, which served as an operating table. This was typical of the difficulties he encountered in his work.

There was a crying need for dentistry. Many gunshot

wounds were dressed, and several pneumonia cases were discovered. Often Grenfell and his fellow physician were forced to serve as cooks and nurses, since no one capable of doing so was at hand, and he also ordered the supplies for these trips to the lonely settlements as no one knew what was needed. In all, the winter proved highly successful, and the doctors traveled by dog sled more than fifteen hundred miles on this mission of mercy.

Returning to Battle Harbor in time for spring, he found the new hospital ship, the *Strathcona*, riding at anchor, and in this vessel Dr. Grenfell made his summer cruises along the Labradorian coast. He visited the Moravian stations again, and as the brethren wanted to find a site for a new mission, he took one of them to Cape Chidley. Here in this northern end of Labrador the doctor found cruising delightful.

He stood amazed as the boat rode at anchor below the great Appalachian Mountain range which here runs out to the water's edge and forms a seafront of embattled cliffs towering two and three thousand feet. Narrow passages cut deep into the mountains that are old valleys which the glaciers in the long-lost past have scooped out. The precipices are steep and weather-worn, yet covered with lichen and other Arctic plants.

With winter near, the doctor longed to stay at St. Anthony, and so, with an old friend from the Hudson Bay Company, he settled down to continue the previous year's work. He was able to arrange with the government for a medicine payment of twenty-five cents to be used for patients who could not afford this fee; thus the financial burden was lifted somewhat. The needs for a permanent hospital again impressed him, and finally he challenged a hundred men to go with him, by dog sled, for a couple of weeks into the timbers, from which they returned with sufficient lumber for a thirty-six-foot-square building. Thus the dream of a hospital at St. Anthony began to become reality.

During this time Dr. Grenfell served as a justice of the peace, and one of his duties was to handle problems arising out of the truck or bartering system of trade. Here at St. Anthony the people told him how the traders cheated them. During this Newfoundland visit the doctor stayed with a young minister who previously had been a trader but because of the abhorrent "truck" system had left the work. In the evening when friends visited the doctor and the minister, they discussed the feasibility of forming a co-operative store or trading center.

The fishermen told how they were forced, through fear, to bring their catch to the trader and barter their merchandise for whatever he was willing to offer. They were afraid to trade elsewhere or seek better bargains, for often in such situations the trader would terminate dealings with them. The doctor heard of one man who had sold a small part of his catch to another in order to get milk for his children, only to find that when hunting time came again, the merchant refused to sell him powder, and the customer was thus unable to obtain game for food.

The fishermen were virtually slaves to the traders, and the penalties were almost unbelievable as the stories poured into the doctor's ears. The minister eventually agreed to assist the missioner in organizing a co-operative store on the Newfoundland side of the straights. When the meeting date arrived, the folk gathered from neighboring settlements at a small village fourteen miles north of St. Anthony. The minister, fearing the traders, at first refused to attend, but when his dog driver was sent for him, he came. However, he threw his influence entirely on the side of the old system and its evils.

On the way to the village gathering, Grenfell's sled and dogs fell into the open waters as he crossed a small bay, but borrowing dry clothes, he managed to appear. While

the meeting was being opened with prayer, the hundreds
of sled dogs that had hauled the people from the various
settlements howled dismally outside. Calling upon God
to bless the venture, Grenfell gave information on prices,
debts, statistics and the blessings of co-operative stores
elsewhere. The meeting house was crowded to overflowing
with fishermen afraid to open their mouths because they
feared the traders' reactions against them.

Hence Dr. Grenfell and the traders were virtually the
only speakers. However, one old fisherman eventually said,
"Doctor— I means Mr. Chairman—if this copper store
buys a bar'l of flour at St. John's for five dollaws, be it
going to sell it we fer ten? That's what us wants to know."

Pandemonium broke loose as the meeting came to a
close. The general opinion seemed so united against the
traders that the people thought there must be something
commendable in the co-operative store venture. Finally a
fisherman popular with the people agreed to manage the
new venture. Though unable to read, write or even do
simple sums, he was respected and beloved of the fisherfolk, and with him as director, the new store was started.

Later another store was opened at Flowers Cove somewhat to the west of St. Anthony. The minister heartily
joined in the work, as did nearly everyone in the settlement. This store proved a success and ten-percent dividends
were reaped on the investment. Other stores were established both in Newfoundland and Labrador, some successful, others failures, though all had a beneficial effect on the
community, since they stimulated initiative. One store
opened near Battle Harbor did $60,000 worth of business
the first year and aroused the violent enmity of the traders,
who appealed to the government and secured a commission
to look "into the mission as a menace to honest trade."
Nothing, of course, came of the charge.

Dr. Grenfell, writing of the truck, or barter, system, said
that since the people traded or bartered their fish and furs

to the trader, at the latter's valuation, they had little conception of their products' worth. They did not know the value of the fish they caught or the price of the things they were buying. At one time the doctor became so discouraged by the malnutrition and disease of the children and the adults that he made a trip to British Columbia and entered into an agreement with the prime minister to send two hundred Labradorian families to sites selected on that seaboard, "he to advance the passage money and see that they got a fair start."

The Newfoundland government refused to aid the project, but Grenfell continued to champion it until at length "we started a cash co-operative store, we at once becoming anathema." It was this which aroused the investigating committee, who were seeking to criticize the economic and moral policy of the doctor. Nothing came of the efforts of the group, headed by the traders, for the people soon saw the advantage of managing their own business affairs.

In this, as in other ventures for the welfare of the people, the divine blessings were upon Grenfell and his co-laborers as they sought to tell the fisherfolk of Christ, the Saviour from sin.

# Chapter 6

# *TRIALS AND TRIUMPHS*

WHEN CHRIST CALLED Grenfell to Labrador, the doctor was challenged to rebuild the entire life of the fisherfolk. As the years passed, the God-guided missioner had a solution ready for every problem. This demanded ability to withstand criticism and often meant the loss of the Board's co-operation. But God always furnished new friends when old ones failed or lost interest. Grenfell loved the people he served, and he desired to give them advantages which hitherto had been denied them.

When the co-operative stores began to prosper, Grenfell turned his attention to a phase of work which had been neglected. Throughout the St. Anthony section was much valuable timber, sufficient to run a sawmill, but when the physician studied the asset-liability sheet of the sawmills he found that they were not paying ventures. He determined, therefore, to utilize the cheap labor at hand and enter the timber business. This involved employing the fishermen who otherwise had little if anything to do in the wintertime, so that whatever they earned would be "plush," to use an expression common among them.

When the suggestion was submitted to the Mission Board, the Council quickly passed it back to the doctor. They were more interested in spiritual values and soul building. He must handle other matters. Hence the venture was his own, even the financing, management and disposal of the output, except as the government furnished a small subsidy. The government was interested in aiding the support of the needy in that region, and felt that if the sawmill would achieve this end, the investment would be worth it.

Grenfell had always been strong in faith, and operating the timber business by faith was no different from building a hospital through faith, furnishing a hospital and mercy ships through faith, finding suitable volunteer doctors, nurses and teachers through faith. Believing he could trust God to sustain him, Grenfell launched forth.

One problem vexed him not a little. He could not afford to be absent from his northern cruises during the summertime, while the mills were being constructed, as there seemed to be no one else available to oversee this work. But through faith he provided two English friends as volunteers to help, and even furnished their transportation.

When the proper surveys of timbers, locations available and workmen needed were checked, the work began to take form gradually. Houses built and supplies garnered. A little schooner, the *Co-operator*, used by the co-operative stores, brought the machinery to the selected site. At times, as the doctor cruised in the far northern waters, he wondered how the mill was progressing, for he knew that many problems, especially that of transporting the heavy machinery, of which the boiler was the largest, would confront the overseers. There was no wharf at St. Anthony where all these supplies could be unloaded, and the *Co-operator*, as he believed, was not large enough to carry it. There was nothing he could do, no advice he could offer. Radios and airplanes were undreamed of, but the avenue to the skies was opened and through prayer he communicated with heaven.

When snow began to fly and ice covered the waters, he was able at long last to visit the enterprise. On a wooded promontory, rising above a deep harbor, was a cluster of small huts, and here he found the home of the new project. The boiler, by some feat of skill had been landed, and the two young Englishmen, full of confidence and strong in faith, were active in carrying the plans to fruition. All was going well, the missioner-dreamer found to his delight.

By spring the heavy saws were humming their way through the timbers and piles of lumber were stacked about, evidence that the fishermen had been busy at the mills. The second winter was more trying than the first, for many of the lumber buyers had merely put their charges on the books and the bills were not paid. Hence money was not at hand to carry the logging fishermen through the winter as Grenfell desired, nor could funds be borrowed on so uncertain a venture, destined, apparently, for failure. This proved a test of the missionary's faith, and calling upon God, he found the strong arm of the Almighty sufficient to carry even this burden.

Years later the doctor saw the wisdom of forming a contingent fund, called the Discretionary Fund, for such emergencies. This consisted of money contributed, the disposal of which was left to the missionary. But at this time, no money was available, and Grenfell furnished the necessary cash.

In God's own time the money arrived, but so late in the season that the delivery of supplies became a major problem, for the entire bay was ice-choked. The *Strathcona,* bringing the goods ashore, became ice bound and could not butt its way through, but the doctor was undaunted.

He found excellent marble near by, and later he induced an English company to develop the industry in a small way. This became a start in the utilization and development of natural resources, all of which improved living conditions. The sawmill continued to prosper, and gave employment to the workmen beside furnishing lumber for homes and public buildings such as schools and churches.

During the long winter months the fishermen spent their time fur trapping, and the doctor, studying the handicaps under which they worked, reached the conclusion that something must be done to make this more profitable. Since the fisherman did not realize enough from their catches, either of fish or fur-bearing animals, they had to rent their traps from the traders, and consequently their furs were on a share basis. In this respect they resembled the share-croppers of the deep South.

The doctor, surveying these terrible conditions, decided that fur farming could be made successful, and at the same time remove the hazards of fur trapping. Often the trappers were caught in severe blizzards or suffered other mishaps on the trail. Dr. Grenfell selected a site near the St. Anthony hospital and bought a dozen pairs of fur-bearing foxes. He set out to raise furs on a semiscientific basis, and the people became greatly interested in the experiment. In fact, those wishing to see the captive animals soon wore a deep path to the farm.

However, the project did not prove a success, and the experiment was discontinued, though in later years, fur farms sprang up throughout Newfoundland and Labrador. The Hudson Bay Company developed a huge farm, and on Prince Edward Island, fur farming became an important industry. Although the doctor failed in his local venture, it was he who initiated this type of work elsewhere. The failure of the experiment was not caused by the fact that fur farming could not be carried on profitably, but because of the lack of proper handling, oversight and leadership. Later, mink breeding was begun, and a survey of its possibilities for Labrador was made in 1932 by Professor Darling of Edinburgh.

Always alert to conditions, Grenfell knew that sooner or later he would be called upon to face another emergency, that of caring for Labradorian orphans. On an early visit along the coast, while he was stopping at a small village where the people faced starvation because they were so deeply in debt to the trading schooner that more credit was impossible, someone entrusted two orphan children to his care. They owned absolutely nothing; even their clothes had been borrowed from others. When Dr. Grenfell sailed away, the children were his wards. Later, on another trip, he came to a lonely log house where he found the mother lying on the floor dead, the father dying on a rude board couch and five forlorn children crammed into a corner awaiting the lot which they knew would be theirs. The next day both parents were buried and since there was no one else to shoulder the children's responsibility, they became the missioner's charge. At another place where the doctor's boat dropped anchor, a woman came aboard with two bundles under her arm—two tiny babies.

"Something wrong with them," she said simply, after unwrapping them and laying the infants on the table.

Investigation showed them to be blind, and the woman, whose husband had been killed a short time before, found it impossible for her to care for them. Consequently she gave the babies to the doctor.

Thus a children's home came into existence. As soon as it was noised abroad that Dr. Grenfell was caring for orphaned and destitute children, they came to him. Ragged, dirty, half-starved, destitute, even unclothed, they came to Dr. Grenfell. Some were crippled; others were diseased. One tiny girl of four was without legs. Her limbs had been frozen and were gangrenous, so her father had chopped them off with an axe. In the home she was faithfully cared for, and was later fitted with artificial legs. As time passed, she learned to walk so well that few were aware of the fact that she had two artificial legs.

The consecrated missionary built the first home in northern Newfoundland, and as the need increased, others were erected in Labrador. The first building was constructed of green timbers, which contracted with the heat in the building during the winter, with the result that there were leaks in the roof and large holes in the walls. Bitter winds from the North Pole rattled the windows, tiny white mountains of snow were on the floors. This demanded a concrete building, more easily heated, and winged so that boys and girls could have separate sections in which to live.

The inventive doctor decided to construct this new building of concrete blocks, called bricks, priced at twenty-five cents a "throw" and for which he could ask donors to pay. Soon enough bricks were sold, and under the leadership of William Delano, director of the mission, and president of the Architects' Institute, the building took form. Friends gave furnishings, patrons provided memorial beds, memorial rooms, and the work was finished cost-free by local helpers. During the summer, students from Princeton, with the aid of Professor William Gillespie, came during their vacation and put in the foundation. Women volunteers stepped forward to assist in the management of the home.

The needlework Guild of America and similar groups sent clothing and other needed articles. Today several of these institutions dot the desolate shores, where they performed their work of transforming neglected, homeless and suffering children into healthful, energetic and useful boys and girls.

The doctor saw another opening for Christian service. Often he discovered unusually intelligent Labradorian young people who needed educational advantages thus far denied them.

Said a sixteen-year-old Scotch lad to the doctor one

day as the hospital ship was tied up at a wharf, "I'll work ten hours a day as a carpenter, for I am able to do this kind of work, if you will give me one hour a day of teaching." The young man did not seek medicine, nor did he request financial aid. He sought only to barter his carpentry for education.

The doctor acted upon the boy's suggestion, and eventually the Pratt Institute granted him a scholarship. Years later it was he who superintended the construction of the first reinforced concrete hospital building, complete with electric lights, modern plumbing and all the equipment essential to an up-to-date hospital. During his school days he learned to play the organ. Later he became a government surveyor, supervised the Grenfell operations, served as director of the co-operative stores and, as a hobby, directed the wireless station of the mission.

Grenfell viewed this agreement with the lad as one of his most profitable bargains.

The doctor was intensely interested in the education of the isolated sections of his territory, where there was little hope of popular education for the masses. Hence the children grew up in illiteracy, except where mission stations and occasional government-sponsored schools brought learning to them.

At first Dr. Grenfell tried to combine the local St. Anthony schools into one free public school, but this terminated in failure caused by prejudice and even sectarianism. Consequently he decided to provide a building himself and plan a future educational program. Friends quickly subscribed three thousand dollars for the venture. The Pratt Institute blueprinted the building and Labradorian boys did the work. Teachers volunteered their services since there was no money to pay them. Textbooks were also donated, and in the large upper hall of the building was a thousand-volume library. Here also was a place for entertainments and drills.

On one of his trips Dr. Grenfell was perturbed by the lack of toys and games to engage the children's free time, and he determined to do something about it. Among his volunteer teachers he found one who introduced organized play, and quickly the children seized the opportunity.

Of course, there was soon opposition to this nonsectarian school and its up-to-the-minute methods. Parents were told that if their children attended the new school they would be unable to pass colony examinations, and hence would not be eligible for government positions. Fortunately, while this rumor was raging, a Chicago patroness furnished an endowment fund which made teacher-training possible, and introduced as well the colony curriculum, so that the pupils passed the legal examinations. Thus many of them in later years served responsible teaching positions and other governmental posts.

Dr. Grenfell, always eager to serve his Lord and Saviour, was exceedingly practical, and as occasion demanded or inspiration provided, he introduced instruction in weaving, loom work, carpentry and other crafts. Funds were also provided which made possible the sending of the mentally energetic and capable students to other institutions for higher training. The Pratt Institute of New York City, long a friend of the Labrador doctor, provided scholarships for higher technical training and social contacts with modern civilization outside the narrow confines of those along northern coasts.

Sailing along the lonely coastline, dipping deep into the bays and fjords, the doctor of Labrador discovered remote settlements and homes where mail steamers did not come, and with no hope of educational facilities. Dreaming, praying, visualizing the needs, the thought leaped to his consciousness that he must provide instruction for these people in the out-of-the-way places of the world. Soon, under the inspiration of his prayers, Ethel Muir, a long-time teacher holding a doctor's degree, stepped forward and offered her services for the summer teaching.

So successfully did she travel among the settlements and live off the country, that other teachers volunteered. These workers lived with the fishermen and daily conducted classes of adults and children. Clergymen, struck by this Christian service, praised their work, and the superintendent of education for the colony said that this was one of the mission's most beneficial and humanitarian phases or service.

Thus the educational program came into being and as the decades passed, schools began to dot the land. The original St. Anthony school now has a large enrollment. Some of these institutions have been supported and even conducted by students from leading American universities, including Yale and Princeton. The Lockwood School at Cartwright, for instance, was the gift of a Texas woman, and is one of the mission's most prosperous institutions.

Always on the alert for new methods and schemes of helping the land he loved, he called the government's attention to the disastrous lack of lighthouses, but nothing came of his efforts. However, one day he told several of his friends about the need for a lighthouse near the Battle Harbor hospital, and they subscribed funds for the venture. An architect drew up the plans, and another supporter furnished money for the lighthouse keeper's salary. Construction was about to begin when the government suddenly forbade the work to be carried forward.

The Labrador doctor was told that lighthouse building and tending was in the government's sphere of power, and hence not under the jurisdiction of private individuals. However, to ease the doctor's disappointment, they informed him that already funds had been voted for the erection of the lighthouse at Battle Harbor, and in a short time the friendly light and guiding rays of Double Island

Lighthouse beamed across the waters, guiding many boats to the haven of the bay. Other lighthouses were erected at Indian Ticker, Indian Harbor, White Point and other points up the coast.

The tireless servant of Christ found also another field wherein he could be of service. As he visited the people's isolated huts, he discovered that food was always a scarsity. He saw that in Lapland the reindeer were serving not only as beasts of burden, but were also providing food, clothing and shelter, so he decided to introduce reindeer husbandry among his people. A herd of three hundred was shipped from Lapland, and along with them came shepherds or herders, all of which were put ashore three miles south of St. Anthony, where the climate was suitable for the animals.

Much to Grenfell's delight the herd increased rapidly. All would have gone well had not the Lapp herders become weary of being separated from their homefolk and clamored for a raise in wages. At first their demands were met, but time and again they asked for more pay until the burden became too great for the doctor to bear. Dr. Grenfell finally decided that he would use local helpers, some of whom had been trained by the Lapps. But "No Lapps, no deer," was the warning.

For some time under Newfoundlanders the deer did well, increasing in number. The cheese made from the milk was delicious, the meat appetizing. Some of the deer were sold to the Canadian government for the Peace River section, but with them went the chief herder and two of his experienced assistants. Caring for the remainder of the herd proved a problem, as those who had this responsibility became lax in their duties. The people grumbled about the fact that the deer destroyed their gardens, and others complained that the animals endangered life. Some deer were stolen and slaughtered; others sickened and died.

Finally an offer came for their purchase, and eventually all were sold.

Even after this experience, Grenfell continued to maintain that the North country was the place where herds could profitably be maintained, since there was useless land stretching thousands of miles which could be used for grazing deer. He said further that land over which the deer had grazed produced more grass the following years than before, and since no other domesticated animal could endure the cold, the deer was a profitable source of milk, meat, clothing, transportation and even pleasure for those in that bleak land.

Although Grenfell accepted the fact the venture was a total failure, he believed strongly in the lesson he had taught those who controlled the future of the North. When deer were later introduced into Alaska, Grenfell's experiment paid dividends, and the Labrador failure became an Alaskan success. Not always did the doctor see immediate results from an idea he introduced, but often the seed he sowed bore fruit in other sections of the world.

Not once did he waste an opportunity to improve the conditions of Labrador, for he was constantly seeking means by which to uplift living among the people. He even introduced various kinds of seed which had been used in other cold regions, and thus gardens and crops could be raised more profitably.

Meanwhile Dr. Grenfell's hospital work, as well as that of his schools, progressed. A new wing, a convalescents' room and an enlarged operating room were added to the Battle Harbor hospital. The hospital at Indian Harbor was also expanded.

He was struck one day by the lonely lot of isolated families who lived in remote regions, and as a consequence he organized a society for sending literature and letters to them. This afforded cheer and inspiration to the groups thus contacted. At Grenfell's suggestion, Andrew Carnegie furnished several small portable libraries which were distributed along the coast. Thus, in various ways, the Grenfell spirit and energy battled ignorance, poverty and suffering along the frozen shores of the Atlantic.

God was with Grenfell, and as he prayed, he constantly pleaded for divine guidance. Grenfell was a missionary who sought to heal bodies, but he did not forget the souls, the minds and the spirits of the sufferers.

# Chapter 7

# THE GIRL IN BLACK

LONG BEFORE the mission had become the Labrador Medical Mission, the work was already linked closely with Dr. Grenfell. The world looked upon Labrador as his special sphere, and he loved that land of ice and cold. During the early part of this century, Canadian secretaries had kept the needs before the public.

In New England a loyal worker started an organization with a board of directors, and, from a central office, published pamphlets telling of the Labrador doctor's Gospel labors and industrial activities. For some time Dr. Grenfell felt that it would be wise to consolidate this publicity so that the work might be better known throughout the English-speaking world. It was his desire to tell others of what he had been able to accomplish through Christ's assistance that his burdens might become theirs and through their prayers and financial assistance they might share his load.

Consequently it was decided to publish a quarterly magazine entitled *Among the Deep-Sea Fishers*. The purpose of this publication was the disseminating of information concerning the mission, winning friends for the cause and assisting in securing needed contributions to enlarge the boundaries of the mission. Julia Greenshields, a Toronto friend, promised to edit the magazine and also to assume responsibility for possible financial losses.

The doctor had been called upon to appear on platforms throughout England and America, and though he did not like this type of work, desiring rather to be active in easing the physical sufferings of the people he loved, nevertheless he became quite proficient at public speaking. He affirmed that lecturing about Labrador, though he loved the land and the people, was the least romantic task he had ever been called upon to perform. He added, "But in a work like ours, which is not under any special church, funds must be raised largely through voluntary subscriptions," and the lecture platform became a main source of such offerings.

God had greatly blessed the Labrador doctor and the world began to take him to its heart. Here and there, honors were bestowed upon him. In 1907 the old and custom-bound university, Oxford, honored him with the degree of Doctor of Medicine of Oxford, the first time in all its history that this ancient institution had conferred the degree *causa honoris.* Dr. Grenfell appreciated the distinction, and though he said little about it, he was happy that he had labored under the Master in such a way as to attract such attention to the land he served. Later many American universities granted him the honorary degree of Doctor of Laws.

The eye of royalty was also upon him, and King Edward presented him with a Companionship in the Order of St. Michael and St. George (Knight Commander of the Ancient Order of St. Michael and St. George). The honor could either be conferred directly to the person or sent to the recipient, and Dr. Grenfell desired to receive the honor in person. This, he knew, would make it possible for him to meet the king personally. It meant a year's delay, for he was so busy with his Labradorian tasks that he could not leave them. Permission having been granted by the king for him to come the following year, Grenfell looked forward eagerly to the time when he would sit with the nation's leader.

When the occasion arrived, his old friend and teacher Sir Frederick Treves introduced him to the king, and Dr. Grenfell had a most enjoyable meeting with his sovereign, with whom he discussed Labradorian affairs and conditions in Newfoundland. The famous physician looked upon the king's recognition of his work as having value both in Canada and England, for his fellow countrymen viewed the honor as a mark of distinction and prestige.

In the fall of 1908 urgent calls came from England that he return for lectures, since his work was attracting widespread attention. He looked with favor upon the trip since he was eager to see his mother, who was nearing eighty. He planned to return to his work the following spring via the United States, where he would speak at various points and receive degrees from both Williams College and Harvard. In his native land the lectures were well received as he addressed workingmen's clubs and lecture-course audiences.

When departing time came, he dreaded to leave his mother, realizing that it might be the last time he would see her. Knowing that she would be thrilled to see her son receive his degree, he wondered if it would not be possible for her to accompany him to America. They sailed together, son and mother, on the *Mauretania*, where the Cunard company gave her a luxurious suite of rooms, especially furnished for her comfort.

Though his mother was confined to her room most of the time, still Dr. Grenfell had much to engage his attention, for the first day out, a beautiful young woman dressed in black, whom he called "The Girl in Black," appeared on deck, and the doctor was fascinated by her. Suddenly

he thought, *We are racing at the speed of six hundred miles
a day to the end of this journey when we shall part.*

Then for the first time in his life the voice of love
whispered, "Why don't you do something about it?"

And he decided to do something about it. He knew
little about the young woman, only that she was accompanying the Stirling family, of Chicago, who had just
returned from a trip through Europe. On the second day
out, Grenfell awoke to the fact that the voyage would
soon be over, and they would be landing. Until this trip
he had never thought of marriage, so absorbed was he
in his work. He had felt no need of a helpmeet, but had
carried the load alone.

He did not entangle his courtship with the usual verbose meanderings of lovers, but he went directly to the
question, and asked "The Girl in Black" if she would
marry him. Then the girl mentioned that he did not
know her name—a detail he had forgotten.

Blankly the girl replied, "But you do not even know my
name!"

The quick-witted doctor replied, "That is not the issue.
The only thing that interests me is what it is going to be."

The issue was not decided at the moment, for when
the boat landed, their paths were to go in different directions. The busy doctor was faced with numerous speaking
engagements, so he must go his way, and the young lady
must return to Chicago, where she would again take up
abode with her own mother. But it was agreed that when
Grenfell had completed his Labradorian lectures and had
received his degree, he and mother Grenfell would go
to Chicago where he could continue his courtship.

He could not forget beautiful Anne Elizabeth Mac-
Clanahan, the only child of her widowed mother. Anne
had told the doctor something of her parentage. Her
father had been Colonel MacClanahan, a Southerner of
Scotch ancestry who fought under Robert E. Lee in the

Civil War and had been Judge Advocate General on the staff. Losing everything in the Civil War, he had gone to Chicago, where he resumed his law practice. Here he had married Rosamond Hill, the daughter of a popular judge. Anne's brother Kinlock had died earlier, leaving her alone with her mother in Chicago.

She told Grenfell that her family had a beautiful summer residence at Lake Forest, nestled among the trees on a bluff high above Lake Michigan. The Stirlings also had a Lake Forest home, and the doctor made a lasting friendship with this family also. Later Mr. Stirling went to Labrador, where he studied problems and gave valuable aid and advice concerning conditions there.

As soon as Dr. Grenfell had completed his speaking engagements, he and his mother rushed to Chicago where he received Anne's answer and her mother's blessings. The visit was all too short, for the call of Labrador was strong, and the doctor must be back at his accustomed tasks. After selecting November 18, 1909, as the wedding date, he rushed homeward.

During the busy summer which followed, the St. Anthony hospital was enlarged and a new wing was added to the orphanage so that more children might be cared for. At this time Grenfell also had the privilege of entertaining Admiral Peary who stopped at Battle Harbor on his way back from the North Pole. This visit brought no little stir to the mission center, for newspapermen flocked to the place that they might interview the famous explorer. Friends, fishermen and Labradorians came in such numbers that the little town buzzed with excitement. Grenfell greatly enjoyed meeting the members of the expedition and the visiting newspapermen.

When fall came, the Labrador doctor went to Chicago, where the marriage was solemnized in Grace Episcopal Church, and followed by a honeymoon at Virginia Hot

Springs. In January, bride and groom sailed for St. John's, where they took up their work immediately.

Already a home had been built at St. Anthony, and the furniture had been sent during the summer. The doctor had built a home, cheery with broad windows that looked out upon a wooded hill and the sea with its beautiful harbor. When the newlyweds arrived, a huge fireplace was crackling with logs. In the glass-enclosed veranda were deer antlers, snowshoes, fishing rods, and guns.

The doctor, had he searched the world, could have found no one better suited to be his wife than Anne. She was made especially, so it seemed, for the task she assumed. God blessed the union with three children, born at St. Anthony: Wilfred in 1910, Kinlock in 1912 and Rosamond in 1917.

Anne performed the mission work admirably, and was always a gracious hostess to all who visited their home. Workers, traveling visitors, fisherfolk from up and down the coast—all came and went freely. On one occasion fifty-eight enjoyed a Sunday-evening dinner, after the accustomed "sing," and at another time, twenty fishermen sat down to large tables, spread with a bounteous repast, which had been placed on the sun porch.

As an organizer and administrator Anne did most helpful work. Through her efforts the Child Welfare Department and the Educational Fund were established. Each fall she either took personally or made arrangements for someone else to take a number of boys and girls to colleges and schools in Nova Scotia, Canada or the United States, that they might see the advantages of education in lands other than their own. It was no little task to outfit the young people, purchase their tickets, plan the route, and, when necessary, to travel with them. But Lady Grenfell found joy in helping young people.

Some of these young folk became students at various institutions outside of Labrador, and after graduation, they became valuable assistants in the doctor's work. To-day many of them are serving their homeland as mechanical engineers, electricians, plumbers, teachers, artisans of various kinds, nurses, co-operative-store clerks and managers, and other types of workers.

Anne Grenfell was constantly seeking methods arousing the interest of new friends in the work so dear to her heart. She devised money-making plans and methods of which the doctor had never dreamed. She prepared a mission calendar showing the beauties of Labrador, and through the years thousands, even millions, of them have been sold. Realizing that one must not merely start an industry in Labrador but also make plans to dispose of the product, she began to find new trade centers to handle the output. She arranged to sell these industrial goods, fashioned in Labradorian shops, in resort hotel lobbies scattered throughout America and Canada. She also established a Dog-Team Tavern on a Vermont highway to sell tea and other foods to travelers and tourists and to market the fishermen's handwork. The fisherfolk made puzzles and other items which were sold at a profit.

Nor did the beautiful "Girl in Black" fail to aid her busy husband with his clerical work. She took charge of the huge pile of correspondence, read his letters and manuscripts, and organized his notes. She also studied short hand and typewriting.

The doctor wondered how for so many years he had been able to carry on without Anne's aid. He found that his life's horizon was broadened by her companionship, and he believed that "marriage team-work is God's plan for us on earth."

All, however, was not to be smooth sailing for Anne and her Wilfred, for shortly after their marriage a financial calamity fell upon them and wiped out the family fortune. Dr. Grenfell, a broad-hearted doctor, was a planner, a dreamer of great dreams, a man who was able to translate those dreams into concrete and stone. But he was not a financial wizard.

This was evident in the co-operative stores. He organized them, lent them money with which to start, and businessmen, and even the law, thought him financially responsible for their liabilities. Consequently the merchants of St. John's gave them credit—liberal credit. The doctor, busy with his other work, did not investigate the financial status of the stores. He did not trouble himself with balance sheets, profits and losses, but thought this a concern of the managers. In summer he sailed the Labradorian waters, healing bodies and bringing the Gospel to sick souls. In winter his dogsleds plied the boundless snow tracks of the North.

In the summer of 1910 he was rudely awakened from his financial lethargy by the discovery that the co-operatives were forced with a debt of twenty-three thousand dollars. The St. John's merchants held Grenfell personally responsible for the obligations, though he was not a man of wealth. However, he faced the issues with calmness, calling the creditors together and assuring them that he would do his best to liquidate the obligation.

Finally he sold what personal property he possessed, disposed of his investments, and arranged for each store to pay what it could. Eventually all debts, except those of one merchant, were wiped out. Finally this dealer forgave the obligation in a most generous manner.

The doctor did not blame the people for this tragedy, but realized that it had come about because of mismanagement, inexperience and poor bookkeeping. He even assumed responsibility for the failure in that he had not given sufficient oversight to the matters of record keeping, income, outlay and financial status. He always admitted that he had little if any liking for business affairs. After the difficulty was solved, many of the stores continued to do a justifiable business and showed worthy dividends.

They were able to undersell other traders so that ultimately the fisherfolk received benefits from the venture.

About this time a desperate need came to Dr. Grenfell's attention. He had always been heartily interested in the broader lives of the fishermen, knowing that he must not only carry their needs at Labrador, but also elsewhere. Said one of the men to the doctor: "It is easy for the person to tell us to be good, but it is hard on a wet, cold night to be good on the open street."

The doctor saw that in St. John's there was no pleasant place ashore where the men could spend their free time in hospitable and wholesome surroundings. Nor was there a place where the crews of ship-wrecked vessels could be given temporary accomodations.

The doctor found further, that boardinghouses for fishermen were not desirable, and owners of private homes were ofttimes unwilling to welcome the fishermen. Likewise, girls coming to the city from little villages scattered over the island, and knowing no one in town, were at the mercy of the unscrupulous. Dr. Grenfell, always the good Samaritan, and his associates were confident, however, that the Lord would make provision for these folk.

There was no friendly "Y.M." or "Y.W." or similar institution to which they might go, for all philanthropic and religious work was strongly sectarian.

However, Dr. Grenfell did discover an old seamen's home, but on inspecting the building, he found it delapidated and haunted by fishermen who were habitual drunkards. Consulting the trustees, of whom he himself was one, Dr. Grenfell decided that the building should be sold and the funds therefrom derived added to the money for a new building.

The doctor was certain that the new venture would meet with no serious opposition, for he had already suffered many an attack with the whiskey interests, but always had emerged victorious. He expected the present opposition to be stronger and more widespread, but he was accepting his challenge not from men but from God. After much prayer, he was convinced that it was time to build.

The cause was worthy, and Grenfell knew that God would bless and prosper the venture. The very size of the project seemingly assisted the opposition, for reports were circulated affirming that the project was merely food for the doctor's vanity and prestige. Some maintained that a building such as he planned would soon become a white elephant and financial burden.

Said others, "Merchants and townsmen will be asked to support it."

Meanwhile the doctor was making plans, discussing them with civic-minded people, laying the problems before his Heavenly Father, and preparing to step forward when God's hour came. The counterblow was struck by Grenfell who told about the druken seamen and others he had seen wandering through the streets on Christmas morning. He also called attention to the saloons maintained by the city, and mentioned other problems which could be solved by the building project.

As the criticism continued, the missionary decided that a drastic step must be taken, so he laid the entire story before the governor, Sir Ralph Williams, who, though by no means a W.C.T.U. crusader, realized the value of the enterprise to the town and called a civic meeting to convene at the government house. Here he put the plan squarely before the citizens present.

"Will you personally stand for a $200,000 building," he asked, "or a $60,000 building with a $30,000 endowment fund, or for nothing at all?"

They decided to erect a large building, and the task of raising the money was entrusted to Dr. Grenfell. The meeting stirred the townsfolk to action, challenging their imagination, and consequently a business firm provided a site along the main street, while other establishments made large contributions. By 1911, $175,000 had been subscribed, and the project's leaders decided that it was time to lay the cornerstone.

Since opposition had not been overcome, the missionary thought it wise to publicize the project as widely as possible, thus adding to its prestige. Through friends in the homeland he secured the promise of King George, who was to be crowned in Westminister Abbey on the same day, that after the coronation ceremony was completed, the king would press a button which would lay the cornerstone at the little Newfoundland town across the Atlantic.

It was a gala occasion for the crowded city. Flags flew in the breeze as the governor rose to speak, and the bishop of the land offered prayer. When the great moment arrived, the group was hushed as the signal leaped from the wires indicating that the king was ready for his part of the ceremony.

Said the governor solemnly, "We will wait for the king."

Scarcely had his words died when the gong sounded, the national flag leaped upward and the great stone began to move steadily. Cheers tore the air as the cornerstone of the Seamen's Institute was laid at last. Here fisherfolk were to find inspiration and a comfortable home. Here also young girls and women, driven from their island homes by need or desire, were to find spiritual counsel, vocational guidance and assistance in locating employment.

The doctor's achievements were many and great, but the establishment of the Seaman's Institute was perhaps the greatest of them all.

# Chapter 8

# "TO THE MEMORY OF THREE NOBLE DOGS"

THERE WERE MANY thrilling episodes about which Dr. Grenfell told his wife Anne, but one adventure in particular, which had brought him nearer death than any other, always held his audience spellbound when he was in mood for storytelling.

He was a lover of animals, but three noble dogs held first place in his heart. Often he owed his life to a dog-sled so constructed as to catch falling objects. A sturdy ship had often been his means of deliverance. Sailing the uncharted seas through fogs as thick as soup, without a chart, and with only his sense of direction to guide him safely on the homeward course, he experienced dangers untasted by armchair adventurers.

Often he skirted rock-bound coasts, and frequently he barely escaped the hidden reefs in treacherous uncharted bays, and numerous times as, during his days in Labrador, he traveled thousands of miles, only the dog team pulled the doctor and sled out of the storms.

A hand higher and stronger than his own was guiding his destiny, and bringing him to the desired haven. Many were the hours spent in prayer for a safe journey, and

each morning before starting on a dangerous sailing trip
the doctor and his wife sought God's blessing and guidance.

> My God, my Father, while I stray
> Far from my home on life's rough way,
> Oh, help me from my heart to say,
> "Thy will be done!"

Often in the earlier days of their marriage, Anne stood
beside the bronze tablet marking the St. Anthony home and
read the words engraved thereon:

> To the Memory of
> Three Noble Dogs
> MOODY
> WATCH
> SPY
> Whose Lives Were Given
> For Mine on the Ice
> April 21, 1908

One day she asked the doctor to tell her the story of
the dogs' supreme sacrifice that he might live.

"It was on Easter Sunday, April 21, 1908," he told
his new wife as she stood before the bronze tablet in honor
of the dogs' sacrifice. "I was returning to the St. Anthony
hospital when a boy came running to me with the news
that messengers had arrived from about sixty miles to the
south, wanting me to come at once, for a young man was
at the point of death."

Then, taking an easy seat before the broad fireplace
blazing with huge logs, he continued to tell Anne of that
race against death. Late into the evening the story continued, and when it was finished, a prayer of thanksgiving
for the Heavenly Father's care rose from their hearts.

Two weeks earlier, so the doctor told his wife, he had
operated on a young man, but on returning home, the
patient had not received proper care, and a leg amputa-

tion seemed imminent. The men urged the doctor to rush to the scene before the suffering patient died.

Sensing the urgency of the case, Dr. Grenfell seized his black satchel, dressed in an old football suit which he had used twenty years earlier, and hitching his dog team to the sled, he started on the trail of hard-packed snow and ice. The distance was long and the case urgent, and the doctor, realizing that speed was essential urged his team on. Since it was still winter in this tip of northern Newfoundland, the snow was deep. He knew his animals were strong, intelligent, and had sledded him thousands of miles during the winters past, so he was confident that this mercy trip could be successful.

He looked upon a call for aid as a divine summons to go. Grenfell knew that he was not commanded to come back, but merely to go. He entrusted the outcome to the Master, who promised, "Lo, I am with you alway . . ."

Since his dogs were fresh and those of the messengers worn out by the sixty-mile trip to the doctor, he soon outdistanced the other team, which necessitated his waiting for them twice on the trail, and he arrived long ahead of them at the little village where all were to stay for the night.

They stopped on a bay which they had to cross the following morning. When day dawned, he sent his companions on ahead two hours earlier than he took the trail, and he arranged to meet them at a hut across the bay. During the night, rain and fog swept in from the ocean. This softened the snow, broke the layers of surface ice and increased the hazards of dogsledding.

Much to his horror, when it was time to leave the next morning, the rain began to fall harder. This did not daunt him, for the Master's call for help had come, and he must go. For some distance he hugged the shoreline, but finally he came to what seemed a safe ice-bridge leading straight into the heart of the bay to an island about three miles distant.

He knew that if he could reach the island it would be only another four miles to the other shore and this would save a long and arduous trip around the edge of the bay, treacherous with jagged ice and broken floes. Chasms yawned beneath the sled runners as he neared the island, but the strong dogs dashed through to safety and reached the island haven at last.

But four more miles lay ahead before Dr. Grenfell came to the mainland. Looking toward the land, he saw that he faced another and more dangerous type of route, for the solid frozen surface of the sea had broken into ice pans, and these were jammed into a semi-solid mass. The surface was rough and jagged, but it seemed safe to to take the risk. Dr. Grenfell, throwing himself face downward on the sled, mushed the dogs on at top speed.

The team raced away and had almost reached the land when suddenly the winds died and immediately the ice pans began to shift positions, leaving great holes through which the open sea glittered. The wind had crammed the pans together until they made a roadway, but once released, they drifted apart. The surge of the bay broke up the floes, and when the missionary poked the slush with his whip handle, he discovered that only a thin layer of ice kept him from sinking at that instant. His handle went through to the waters below.

His senses reeled. If ever he had faced death, it was now. The path to the island was blocked, and the route forward to mainland was a treacherous trail. The doctor saw the ice disintegrating around him, that on which he and the team stood was rapidly disappearing beneath their feet.

His mind gripped the promise, ". . . *I am with thee even unto the end . . .*" he flung off some of his clothes, threw himself beside the sled and urged the dogs to mush forward, hoping that their burst of speed would carry them over the shallower ice surfaces. Soon, however, the trail-wise dogs sensed their danger and stood still, instantly plunging sled and doctor into the mass of ice and water.

The dogs, urged by their master's voice, leaped against their traces, only to be dragged back by the submerged sled and plunged into the water. Grenfell, always alert physically, seized his hunting knife, cut the traces and freed the dogs from the sled. The lead dog, freed of his harness, clambered upon a mass of broken ice and snow, and turning, he looked at the other dogs. "His countenance," said the doctor, "looked like he was grinning at them, because of the black and white markings of his face."

After cutting the sled traces, Dr. Grenfell tied the line of the lead dog to his wrist. He pulled this desperately, and he was almost to safety when suddenly the dog turned tail-to and slipped the harness off his head. However, the missionary was able to seize the line of another dog, and finally succeeded in raising himself upon the snow-mass. Slowly, one by one, he hauled the dogs upon this "snow raft," as he termed it.

With a prayer on his lips, he viewed the situation and found that he was safe for the moment, though death seemed inevitable, for rapidly the snow patch was drifting out to sea, and he noticed, to his dismay, that it was quickly melting. Some twenty yards away, separated from him by open water and slush ice, was another floe, thicker and apparently stronger. If he and the dogs could reach it, their chances for survival would be heightened, Grenfell believed. Weighing the possibilities, he decided to make the effort, and trusted God to bring him through.

Taking the dogs' traces, he spliced them together, and thus made a long sealskin line, tough and able to hold his weight. Cutting this in two, he fastened one end of each piece to his wrists and the other end to two dogs. To the back of each dog he tied one of his big sealskin boots, as his coat, cap, overalls and gloves were already lost. He then threw the two dogs into the water. He urged them to swim to the ice block and hoped they would tow him along, but each time the dogs leaped back to his stand, and refused absolutely to make the effort, which alone would save the doctor's life.

The dogs, however, had no intention of leaving their driver's side and the more he tossed them overboard, the more persistently they clamered back again. They seemed unable to understand what the doctor wanted them to do. Finally he realized that they were unable to see the block of ice. As he looked at his little pet spaniel, he decided to try the dog's retrieving stunts, so picking up a chunk of ice, and pointing it at the floe some distance away, he threw it. In a flash the spaniel leaped into the water, and bounding over the thin, shifting slush-ice, he was soon sitting on the floe, a thick fluff of black fur.

The other dogs caught the idea and instantly began paddling through the water to the larger block of ice. Finally when the dogs had made the landing, the doctor took to the water and was soon with the dogs. Thankful to God for victory thus far, Grenfell again studied the situation, but realized that he was still far from safety.

The wind was driving the block of ice out to sea, and on close scrutiny he discovered that what he thought to be ice was merely mushy snow frozen into a mass which would break up in the heavy sea to which they were drifting.

The bitter wind, howling from the shore, made him stiff with cold. Taking the precious hunting knife which he had wisely retained, he cut open his boots and used this warm skin to protect his back. He realized that something more than this must be done or death would soon be upon him. The pan was swirling outward toward the sea, and at the bay's entrance the breakers were threshing huge pieces of ice against the cliffs. He knew that even if he did not freeze to death, the ice cake on which he was standing would not long endure this pounding.

Dr. Grenfell realized that he must die unless he found

some source of heat. Suddenly he thought of his faithful dogs, which had pulled him over many icy miles and through many dangers. He knew that they were willing to do this once more, were ready, in fact, to sacrifice their lives for his. Clutching his hunting knife in his hand, he moved slowly over the tottering ice floe. First he killed Moody, then Spy and last, Watch. Skinning each dog, he wrapped himself in their bloody furs and then he stretched their bodies into a rough windbreak against which he might lean.

He tried to wring the water out of his clothes, and as night came, he checked the drift of the floe toward the breakers which were whipping the bay and grinding the ice into a slushy mass.

His feet became stiff with cold, for the moccasins he wore were soaked through and had frozen. Remembering how the Lapps stuffed their shoes with grass, which served as insulation, he began to unravel the rope of his dogs' harness, and this he stuffed into his footwear. This eased his suffering somewhat and took the keen edge off the pain. Then he dipped the rope into fat from the dogs' intestines, but when the candle wick was formed, he found his matches worthless. Since nothing could be done, he cuddled close to the largest, and now the stiffest, dog and slipped into a fitful slumber. About midnight he shivered himself awake to find one hand frozen.

The moon was up, and he could see the ice pan pushing steadily onward to the sea. Praying for deliverance, he felt the wind veer as though directed by an invisible hand. Finally there was a dead stillness, as though Christ had proclaimed, "Peace, be still." Cheered by this, he went to sleep again. When he awoke, something seemed to tell him—and the suggestion seemed foolish indeed— "Raise a flag . . . a flag!"

Cautiously he cut the meat from the dogs' hind-leg bones, and with the remnants of the rope from the harness, he tied these bones together until he had a pole. Taking his shirt, he fastened it to the top of his flagstaff, if such it could be called, and when dawn came, he began to wave his banner vigorously.

He had worn old football clothes for the trip, clothes he had used twenty years earlier at the university—Oxford running shorts, red, yellow and black stockings, and a flannel shirt. In this attire, minus the shirt and plus the dog skins, he stood on the ice pan and waved a crooked pole made of dog-leg bones, to which a flannel garment was tied.

He smiled as he pictured himself, but he could not dismiss the urge to wave the flag. As he waved, he prayed, and God heard that prayer. Somewhat rested, he was feeling fit and alert. He knew he could hold out for at least another twenty-four hours, and food was near at hand —the skinned, frozen dogs had died that he might live.

He continued to wave the flag, and occasionally he thought an oar flashed in the distance. He thought he saw a small boat rising and falling with the waves, but this, too, could not be, and once he thought he discerned the forms of men on the distant cliffs. But Doubt whispered that this was impossible.

Finally an oar gleamed unmistakably, and then the black form of a boat showed strong and clear against the ice, as he saw a craft pushing its way tediously, but steadily to his rescue. Coming nearer, he made out the form of men, who shouted, "Don't get excited. Stay on the pan where you are."

Since there was little else he could do, he took their advice. As the first man leaped on the floe, neither he nor the doctor could speak, so overcome were they with joy and gratitude. Quickly Grenfell and the dogs were taken on board. The men gave the missionary hot tea, and then the boat was rowed, pushed and dragged over the ice until the rescuers and the rescued reached shore.

At length the story came out. On the previous afternoon, said the spokesman, four men had been on the headland cutting up seal meat which they had cached there. As they started for home, one of them thought he saw something peculiar far out on the ice. Rushing back to the village, they told their tale.

Fortunately, a village fisherman owned a field glass, and hastening to a cliff lookout, he searched the sea for sight of man or beast, whatever the strange object might be. He could make out the form of a man on a drifting floe, and as he told the men of the village what he saw, a rescue squad of volunteers was hastily organized, and when day dawned, the little craft put out to sea. The undertaking was extremely hazardous since without a miracle no craft could survive the pounding of the waves and the grinding of the ice. But determination and love spurred the rowers onward, for word had sped through the village that the castaway was the beloved missioner.

With brave hearts and strong arms they pulled against the oars and fought the rough waters and heaving ice for miles, until at length they drew up safely at the shore. Here the entire village had gathered to welcome the seafaring men. As soon as possible, Dr. Grenfell returned to St. Anthony. As he was taken to the hospital on a sled, he resembled a log, for his feet were so badly frozen that he could not use them.

In a short time he had recovered from the ordeal and was back again at his accustomed tasks. As always, he feared no danger either on land or water. He knew that God had work for him to do, and that work would be accomplished.

As he told Anne, the inscribed bronze tablet was placed in loving memory of the three dogs who had died that the doctor might live.

Many were his narrow escapes through the years, but none brought him so near death. Cruising the rocky coasts, which were often treacherous with fog, was not a pleasant and safe task, yet he never hesitated when duty called. Nor were his dog-team trips less hazardous, for there were unexpected blizzards, and often the trail markers were entirely blotted out and accidents there were disastrous on the lonely snowbound trails of the wilderness.

He was confident that God would send deliverance, and he was ever willing to obey his Heavenly Father in whose work he was engaged.

His lecture tours provided a different type of experience. They afforded contacts with delightful people whom otherwise he would never have been permitted to know. But these speaking engagements taxed his strength and requested more energy than the Labradorian hardships. Every night he was in a new city, found a strange audience, and was in an unfamiliar home. Nevertheless he was willing even to undergo these hardships for the sake of his beloved land of ice and snow.

Frequently he traveled from the Atlantic to the Pacific, from Florida and California to Canada. He was engaged to deliver many famous addresses, among which were the Earle Lectures, given at the University of California, where it was the author's privilege to hear Dr. Grenfell speak. Through these lecture engagements at universities and colleges the famous doctor gained many volunteer students for summer work.

During one season he spent six weeks touring Canada, and spoke in a different place each night. He made a similar tour of England where he met old friends and visited clinics, experiences which helped him greatly in the Labradorian medical work. On these trips his wife, beautiful Anne, accompanied and relieved him of many tedious details, cared for the mail, and, when possible, saved the doctor the necessity of talking to prying visitors.

With these engagements came many strange experiences. On one occasion when he was speaking to a man and a woman, neither of whose names he knew, as he attempted to introduce them, he said, "Let me present . . ."

"Oh, never mind," said the man. "We have been married for thirty years!"

Another time Dr. Grenfell was rushing to catch a train after the conductor had shouted, "All aboard." At the train gate he met a man who put out his hand to bar the way. Being accustomed to having people shake hands with him, Dr. Grenfell grasped the man's hand, shook it cordially, and then raced down the platform, followed by the man to the compartment from which the physician's wife was frantically waving to him. The pursuer was the ticket collector.

These incidents enlivened his experiences, and on returning to his Labradorian labors, he enjoyed many a chuckle as he remembered them. He was constantly eager to be about his Master's business, and he believed that both pleasure and trials were from the loving hand of his wise Heavenly Father.

He watched his work prosper beyond his fondest dreams, for he had consecrated his all to accomplishing the mission he set out to perform, to bring Christ to the settlements of Labrador.

# Chapter 9

## *BLESSED THROUGH THE YEARS*

God had supplied Dr. Grenfell's needs through the years, and prospered the work beyond his fondest dreams. Everywhere the Grenfell name was famous, and friends came forward willing to finance his ventures. Dr. Grenfell was a man with but one goal: the betterment of Labrador. He was constantly conscious of the fact that only God could put foundations under his dreams.

Consequently, units of the Grenfell organization sprang up in various countries, and assistants also came from these lands. The doctor, wanting to insure the permanency of the work, thought that the organization would be more efficient if all these local groups could be centralized in one association, with representatives of each serving on this managerial board.

As he viewed the progress he had made since his first trip under the Mission to Deep Sea Fishermen, he realized that he had gone far beyond the confines of this association, which had helped to send the Gospel and medical aid to fisherfolk. Looking to the United States, he saw numerous friends united in an organization for assisting the Labradorian work. These he appreciated.

Thus the Grenfell work and aim was becoming interna-

tional in scope. Dr. Grenfell therefore decided to merge
the various associations supporting his work into one organization. In 1912 the International Grenfell Association
was incorporated, composed of the Grenfell Association
of America, the Grenfell Association of Great Britain and
Ireland, the New England Grenfell Association, the
Grenfell-Labrador Medical Mission and the Grenfell Association of Newfoundland.

Each of these societies was represented by two members,
sitting on the general council, and with this strong and
unified organization, the Grenfell work went forward more
rapidly than ever. Behind every move for the betterment
of Labrador was Dr. Grenfell, the man of towering moral
and spiritual strength. It was he who gave impetus to this
great movement to improve the social and economic
life of those who lived in the desolate land.

Labrador looked to him as its spiritual father. Although not a mighty preacher, he conducted many religious
services. The lads he had won to Christ went out into the
world to become men of action, blessed and used of God.

Dr. Grenfell was the banker, financial authority, economic expert, and family physician for this land of lonely
settlements and bleak shorelines. His personality and
energy were important in the development of hospitals,
children's homes, schools, and churches which were established in the towns and settlements.

The doctor had long prayed for an endowment by which
he might be free from the constant burden of financial
need. One of the Association's first tasks was to raise an
endowment fund. When this decision was made, a decision
believed to be guided by God, the First World War broke
out, and though the time did not seem propitious, still
the endeavor was successful.

An American man, who made such fund-raising his
life's business, was secured to manage the plan, and, with
his family, he moved to Labrador at his own expense to

study the problem and acquire data for the campaign. The undertaking proved successful and as a beginning, sufficient funds were secured to relieve workers and directors of much financial anxiety. Through the years this fund has been generously increased.

Dr. Grenfell could not resist the urge to take an active part in the war. Consequently, in 1915 he joined the Harvard Surgical Unit at a base hospital in France. His Labradorian experiences helped him greatly in treating "trench feet" and other ills arising from cold and dampness.

He also produced a valuable paper, which found its way to the British Medical Journal, on making rain-and windproof material so that the clothing would prevent body heat from escaping at wrists, ankles and similar places.

After the war, he sped back to his beloved Labrador where the work began to expand in numerous ways as he met new challenges in this old field. His original aim, to bring medical assistance to the people, continued to be the dominant idea, and this was achieved most satisfactorily through the coming years. St. Anthony became the headquarters for the work, and the hospital at this place had brought many other projects, such as the children's home, machine shops, storehouses and employment of various types, all of which were factors in increasing the town's population.

Southward about halfway to St. John's was a new hospital at Twillingate. Both the St. Anthony institution and this one were awarded the Grade A certificate when inspected by a representative for standardization from the College of Surgeons of America. This delighted Dr. Grenfell, who believed that only the finest was good enough for his land.

As God blessed the work, hospitals were erected about a hundred and fifty miles apart, and nursing stations for maternity and emergency cases were established between the hospitals. Thus, up and down the coast, in addition to the St. Anthony, Twillingate, Battle Harbor and Indian Harbor hospitals, were medical stations at such places as Harrington, Northwest River, Cartwright, Pilley's Islands, Spotten Islands, Flowers' Cove, Mutton Bay, Hatter's Cove, Conche and other points. This made the condition of the sick and injured quite different from that when Dr. Grenfell first arrived in Labrador.

With the hospitals came churches, their spires reaching to the skies, and their message of Christ ringing throughout the land. A Brooklyn donor provided a stained-glass window for one of these churches. The window was the first of its kind in that region and became an object of delight and inspiration to the many who came to see it.

As the work progressed, Dr. Grenfell felt the pressing need for electric power. Considering the possibility of hydro-electric power to furnish heat, light and power, he knew that harnessing the water supply would greatly reduce the cost of the project. A friend in Rochester, New York, who was intensely interested in the Grenfell idea, generously supplied the money, and a plant was built at Cartwright, the construction work being done by volunteers. Later a concrete-block powerhouse was built at St. Anthony.

The doctor always encouraged initiative among his associates, and thus many blessings came to the work. Some of his plans did not aid Labrador directly, but their benefits to humanity were far beyond the scope of that land. This was true of Grenfell's fur-farming experiment. Although failing locally, it had tremendous implications for the entire world, and today is a highly successful industry.

Indirectly another great blessing came from these fur farms. When the doctor was trying out this venture, John Hays Hammond helped with the experiment by starting a farm near Cartwright. Mr. Birdseye, a young Washington scientist, was placed in charge. On a cold winter day, when the temperature was below zero, Birdseye was catching cod through the ice for his animals, and as he drew the fish out of the water, he noticed that they froze instantly. On reaching home, he thawed them out, and was amazed to see that they were as lively as before. On warmer days, they did not react thus, but were lifeless.

Birdseye's observations led him to investigate the possibilities of fish-freezing and to experiment with the idea. As a result, the Birdseye frozen foods came into existence, and the process is now used throughout the world.

The discovery was a boon to the fishermen whom Grenfell served, for it enabled them to sell their salmon, cod and other fish without boning, salting or even barrelling them. Hence prices were far higher and the overhead cost was reduced considerably.

As the years passed in the early twenties, Dr. Grenfell became convinced that when the fishermen's boats needed repairs, they were wasting much time by having to take them to the extreme southern part of Newfoundland, where the only dry docks were located. Every year he had watched the boats as they were damaged by ice, crushed by hidden rocks or driven into reefs and cliffs by storms. The downward trip was long and tedious and time-consuming. Moreover, the fishermen should have been at their nets, as the trips could be made only in open water.

Dr. Grenfell pondered the possibility of dry docks on the northern part of the island. There were several violent storms. One drove more than forty vessels on the rocks, and another crashed nine upon the shores. These were expensive tragedies. Many of the boats could have been salvaged had repair facilities been near by.

Dr. Grenfell prayed about the need and spoke of it to friends, who soon responded with funds. Doubters wagged their heads over this new "Grenfell folly," as they described it. Through the kindness of an anonymous donor, a first-class dry dock was erected at St. Anthony. It was able to accomodate ships having a keel length of a hundred and fifty feet. Here boats thought to be damaged beyond repair were restored by expert hands and sent out again on profitable careers.

Again the actual construction work was handled by a group of volunteers, so that building costs could be kept at a minimum. In a few years this "Grenfell folly" became a profitable venture, in addition to saving the fishing schooners so vital to their owners.

Having sailed the Labradorian waters for forty years, Dr. Grenfell, always a lover of ships, often longed for suitable navigation charts by which he and others could sail these little-known waters. He knew Labradorian sea-perils as few did. Through his endeavors a few light-houses had been erected, but these were insufficient, and as the years passed, home charts had been made, most of which were the work of Grenfell. But much remained to be done, and the doctor longed to see the Newfoundland and Labradorian coasts charted as accurately as any in the world.

Accordingly he started to collect all available maps and decided to attempt the preparation of a reliable chart.

Everywhere, when he turned for aid, were well-wishers, but there were also opposing groups who blocked assistance. The British Admirality was appealed to, they affirmed that because of international entanglements they were unable to aid the project. The Canadian government, so they declared, would like to have such a completed chart, since they were sending vessels to England via the Hudson Bay route, but legal restrictions prohibited. Wherever Dr. Grenfell went he was confronted with this "sorry-please" attitude. The cost of making such a chart, the missionary doctor knew, prohibited both him and the Grenfell Association from undertaking the project.

This man of God had learned through the years that his Heavenly Father had resources unknown to men, and he felt that now again the mighty power of God was to be revealed.

He learned that Alexander Forbes, a personal friend who was a professor at Harvard, owned both a plane and a power schooner, which he placed at Grenfell's disposal. Other friends donated gasoline and lubricating oil for the work, and a steamship company gave free passage to and from England to volunteer helpers. The Newfoundland government carried all freight free in their steamers and even provided free customs entry and licenses. The New York Geographical Society proffered valuable scientific aid, and the Royal Geographical Society of London also endorsed the project.

In a short time the work was underway. Air surveys were made, and the more important mountains and peaks were scaled. Flights were made to show the possibility and the advantage of using airplanes to carry supplies to trappers and to transport their furs, and, later, for other enterprises as the country developed. Later the British Admiralty sent a steamer, especially equipped for work on the Labradorian coast, to complete the survey.

Consequently Dr. Grenfell had the pleasure of seeing the shore of his adopted country made safe for navigation. Therefore the scenic beauties of the mountains, fjords, waterfalls and rivers of Labrador are now available to tourists. Further, the country's resources are being developed as never before, and the native folk have been provided with new business enterprises.

Dr. Grenfell always believed the resources of Labrador were far more extensive than was commonly believed. He believed, for example, that it was possible to raise vegetables profitably. The season was so very short that vegetables, essential to the health of the people, lacked sufficient time to mature.

"Well," argued the doctor, with his usual foresight, "if the season is too short, make it longer."

When asked what he meant, he replied that the use of greenhouses would extend the length of the growing season. By July, the earliest possible time for planting in the open ground, vegetables raised in greenhouses were already three months old. When these vegetables were transferred to the outside, they were matured by the time of the first frost. He proudly pointed to cabbages which weighed more than eighteen pounds than those produced the first year. As a result, there was a growing demand for hothouse plants, and the following year, fifteen thousand were sold to the local farmers.

The American Garden Clubs donated other greenhouses, and as a result, Labradorian tables boast vegetables formerely unknown to them, and as a result, the health of the people has been improved greatly. The doctor also introduced tree culture in regions where there were no trees. These add greatly to the country's beauty and also form windbreaks which offer protection against the terrific gales which sweep down from the northland.

Looking about for a source of fuel, Grenfell thought of peat, which is abundant in that country. But every experiment resulted in failure, for there seemed no way by which it could be dried and hence made usable. However, it was discovered that when hung in the sun and wind, peat quickly dried so that it could be used for fuel. Agriculture specialists, donating their services, proved that peat mixed with kelp, codfish and seaweed was an excellent fertilizer for gardens.

Dr. Grenfell always found great delight in the study of animals, and he was especially interested in animal husbandry. He realized that the Gospel of Christ met every need of life, and Labrador's problems were no exception. Dr. Grenfell sought to improve the stock of cows, pigs and sheep, and he introduced the raising of bees as a source of foodstuff. He also taught the people how to raise rabbits for food. A friend became interested in the doctor's efforts and donated a herd of eight hundred excellent goats, which provided milk for families who otherwise would have been without this essential food.

An important result of the Grenfell mission was the development of home industries. The fishermen did not seek charity, but only an opportunity to work, especially in the long winter months when their fishing trade could not be conducted, or in those seasons when their catches were small. The doctor sensed this need almost from the beginning—a need as important as the call for medicine, hospitalization and educational facilities. This led to the founding of the industrial department of the missionary work. The making of hooked rugs in homes was already a general occupation, but these were made from drab unattractive garments. If the rugs were to be sold, they must be of new materials and artistic designs.

Volunteers enthusiastically taught the people how to improve their work and use patterns featuring such Labradorian scenes as polar bears, icebergs, dog teams and other local touches, which won many admirers—as well as purchasers—for the rugs. These mats and rugs were also made from silk stockings, and the slogan "When your stockings begin to run, let them run to Labrador," brought many stockings which the Labradorians turned into rugs and sold.

This increased the demand for the products, raised the income of the people and encouraged other types of home industries. Soon the people were weaving homespun cloth, making pottery, constructing baskets and doing excellent bead work, all of which increased the range of activities which engaged their free time and was also an important source of income as the products were sold in a growing number of stores in both Canada and the United States.

Always the doctor's desire was to raise the standard of living. He believed that Christ's Gospel not only saved the souls of men but created an atmosphere in which they could obtain life's highest good. He wanted the people to be prosperous, well-fed, healthy, educated Christians, and with God's help he was achieving these goals.

The men and boys turned their hands to toys, making model sleds, dogteams and other such articles with accuracy and patient design. Carved ivory furnished another material for handwork. The ivory was obtained from walrus tusks and whale teeth, and was carved into miniature chessmen, Eskimos, polar bears, sled dogs and igloos.

Through the twenties and into the thirties, garments called the Kossak, or dickie, was added to the host of salable articles, and it proved exceedingly popular with those who participated in winter sports. This garment is lightweight yet warm. Wind-and rain-repellent, and trimmed with bright embroidery and fur it is extremely picturesque.

The resourceful missionary and his wife gave close attention to marketing these products. Large city stores displayed them, and resort hotels placed them on sale in their lobbies. When a surplus was on hand, a Vermont governor and Henry Ford provided automobiles in which the Labrador Industries took tours and sold the articles made by the people. A Dog Team Tavern opened in Vermont proved an excellent outlet. In England, the goods were displayed at the Imperial Exhibition, which the queen herself patronized.

As the missionary neared the end of his forty years of service in Labrador, he saw a gradual improvement in the people, their homes and their attire.

Dr. Grenfell, always a lover of animals, was a loyal friend of the Labrador dog, used in winter as a means of transportation. The general improvement in conditions, due to his labors, was also reflected in the care which the people gave to the dogs. These teams are important to the life of the people on the coast, since, they furnish transportation throughout the cold season. The people, desperately poor, and often near starvation, were unable to give their dogs proper food.

In some cases the dogs were not only poorly fed, badly housed, but mistreated as well. Dr. Grenfell believed it his duty to teach the people how to care for their dogs. He helped organize dog-team races, and as the fishermen were eager to win, and wanted their dogs in the best possible condition, the project promoted better care of the animals.

Further help was given when a member of the board of the Animal Rescue League offered to build an up-to-date kennel to be used as a model. This type of kennel provided shelter in winter and during the night, and was so constructed that the sea water washed in at high tide and cleansed the kennel. This was an important factor in the improved care of dogs in the coastal area.

During these active and extremely busy years, the Grenfells found time to crowd in two holidays. At the close of 1913 they spent a month traveling in Europe and parts of Asia Minor. Viewing the Coliseum by moonlight, walking up Mars Hill, and tramping over the old scenes of Asia Minor which Paul had visited during his missionary tours proved a valuable stimulus to their work in Labrador.

Dr. Grenfell looked upon Labrador as the God-ordained scene of his labors, and he used every opportunity to give lectures concerning the country to which he gave his life. He was convinced that the Master had called him to these people, and he had little time for interests not related to them and their needs. But in 1924 he was again prevailed upon to make a longer trip around the world. It was, however, only with difficulty that he was drawn away from his first love. But once he had decided to make the trip, he carefully made plans for the extended tour and greatly enjoyed the anticipation of it.

His first travel objective was Egypt, a land which long

had interested him. He and Anne toured Alexandria,
Cairo, Thebes and other historic spots, where they avidly
drank in the centuries which the archaeologist's spade
had laid bare. He decided that Egypt's national anthem
was *Baksheesk*, the beggars' call for hand-outs.

Egypt held particular interest for the physician because
various members of the Grenfell tribe had been associated
with events there. One, an Egyptologist, had excavated
some tombs which Dr. Grenfell christened "the Grenfell
family vaults." Another had discovered the famous *Logos*,
or "Sayings of Christ," in papyrus form, and still another had been in a relief expedition which cost his life.
The doctor and Anne felt led to visit his grave. Coming
away from it, he determined anew to spend himself for his
beloved Labrador, even to give his life for the country
and people so dear to his heart.

A highlight of the tour was their visit to Palestine,
and as they visited the places hallowed by the Master,
their hearts were once more reconsecrated to His service
in Labrador. From the Holy Land they motored across the
Syrian desert, visiting Babylon, the Tower of Babel and
other places of Biblical interest.

"Garbage and dirt everywhere," the doctor said in his
Bagdad notes. "Evil smelling, mean streets. Not a thor-
oughfare through the town except one cleared by the
Germans. Diseases lurking in every corner. To those who
love dirty, polluted corners, dark, blind alleys, suggestions
to every sense of a long, by-gone mediaevalism, we heartily
commend this city."

He delighted in India, for his mother had told him
many things about this land, the place of her birth. The
picturesque villages, the people clad in colorful, though
often ragged, garments, the weird customs—all fascinated
the missionary.

Coming to China, he and Anne sailed up the Yangtze
Kian River for eight hundred miles. They saw beauty

and poverty in strange confusion. Meeting missionaries in these various lands, Dr. Grenfell exchanged experiences with them, and wherever he went he gathered new ideas which he could use in his Labradorian work. Crossing to Korea, where they enjoyed a short visit among these polite people, the Grenfells traveled on to Japan and thence across the Pacific to America. They terminated their around-the-world trip at Labrador, where the doctor again stepped into the harness.

As the doctor looked at Labrador, he was inspired by the tremendous possibilities for his country's future. A chain of mercy stations and hospitals brought relief to the suffering. Churches were telling of Christ and His power to save. The fisherfolk were able to live comfortably from the home and fishing industries. Greenhouses had made possible the raising of vegetables hitherto unknown. Light and heat, the result of hydro-electric power, had made their appearance. The youth of Labrador were being trained in the schools.

Long ago Dr. Grenfell had been thrilled by the possibilities of the land, and now, looking at the past, he had renewed faith in the future.

# Chapter 10

# AT REST ON A LABRADOR HILL

GRENFELL, ALWAYS A BUSY MAN, nevertheless found time to study the world's greatest Book, the Bible, which to him was "a storehouse of all necessary wisdom, an ever up-to-date guide Book." He was first introduced into the glorious mysteries of the Bible at the family altar, when as a toddling babe, then a growing youth and finally a young doctor, he heard his father read the Old and New Testaments in the original. Then he listened as his parent translated the Hebrew and Greek into his native tongue and revealed hidden truths.

This experience at the family altar brought him the joy of reading Scripture from the original and acquainted him with the great events and characteristics of Sacred Writ.

In later years he wrote on the margin of a well-thumbed Bible, one of the many which he wore to shreds during the long years of work in Labrador, "Not to love, not to serve, is not to live." These words had served as a beacon, guiding him across the forty years and more of trials and triumphs in his chosen field of Christian service. They were the motto of this man of God, constantly in contact with human want and suffering, bringing the Master to lonely huts and scattered settlements.

There were other books lining the Grenfell shelves in St. Anthony, but none was so frequently used, so worn by constant reading, as the Word of God. Since the life-transforming night of his conversion in the Moody tent, Wilfred had been a man of one book, for as he had left the tent, someone had given him a copy of the evangelist's *How To Study the Bible.* Grenfell, the young doctor, searching for the truth, had literally taken this book to his heart.

Living in constant contact with God's Word in advising others as to how their lives should be directed, he said, "Study it [the Bible] as a guide to avoid the shoals and rocks, as a key to open the real pathway to life . . . It is the one storehouse of practical truths . . . No mere epistle or collection of epigrammatic truths, no mere book of irreproachable maxims and platitudes, no mythical chronicle of marvels that occurred in a musty past. It is a living storehouse of wisdom."

To this man of God, traveling by dogsled across Labrador's winter snows, sailing its waters in summer, the Bible was the mirror of God's mighty men "who had faced the same difficulties, fought the same battles I have to fight, who tried to overcome but were themselves often vanquished exactly as I am conscious of having tried and failed."

In the Bible he saw prototypes of himself. Herein he shared the road with "weak men like Moses made strong, fainting men like Elijah made courageous, fallen men like David raised up, a Book in which saints are ever made out of sinners; a Book recording an abounding love forgiving sin." He viewed the Bible as a Book "satisfied with faith where my knowledge can't reach," a Book "from cover to cover soaked with and exuding God's abounding love to us His creatures," a Book so written that all men may understand "enough of it to learn love and find salvation . . . yet a Book so profound that it becomes more and more a veritable bottomless mine of wealth, and an unending spring of living water to him who by faith can take it for what it claims to be."

These words, taken from his own book, *What the Bible Means to Me,* reveal how deeply the Bible cut into the marrow of his spiritual life and challenged him to service for the Master.

As the busy doctor trailed the wilderness, lectured on Labrador, the subject dear to his heart, he scribbled notes, often almost illegible, on the margins of his Bibles. In one of his Bibles he placed the words of General Pershing spoken to the American army during the First World War: "Hardship will be your lot." In another was a clipping, quoting Theodore Roosevelt's message to the American troops on June 5, 1917: "What doth the Lord require of thee, but to do justly, and to love mercy, and to walk humbly with thy God?"

He clipped a poem to the pages of one of these Bibles, a poem which had often inspired him as he sought to bring health and hope to the forgotten men of the North:

> Is thy cruse of comfort failing?
> Rise and share it with another
> Scanty fare for one will often
> Make a royal feast for two.

On the flyleaf of another Bible he wrote the names of two men, and scribbled, "My inspirers." These names, George Barrow and Jeremiah Horrox, are virtually unknown to us. Barrow's books, especially *The Bible in Spain,* were among Grenfell's favorites, and he loved to study the thoughts of this man who traversed Europe as a Bible seller, and thus opened many closed hearts to the Word of God.

Horrox was a quiet country clergyman who, in 1640, first observed the transit of Venus. This discovery resulted in an increased interest in astronomy.

On lonely nights as Dr. Grenfell sat in his St. Anthony

home with Anne by his side, he read often of such men of action as Chinese Gordon, Lord Lawrence and Havelock.

One day as he looked into his mirror to shave, he saw a cartoon of the proverbial early bird eating the worm. Anne had often chided him about his early-morning escapades. Many times when fog hung over the harbor, he sped fearlessly through the water, despite the fact that he knew not what moment he would strike an iceberg or a submerged rock.

During the years of his later lecture engagements, Dr. Grenfell was a familiar figure on the American platform. During this time he appealed especially to students, and I recall how, slim and straight, he stood at the University of California and in a none-too-vigorous voice challenged the students to a life of Christian service.

During the late twenties his work prospered. Financial support was liberal, and the market for Labradorian products was excellent, but when the depression came, Labrador and the mission suffered. At this time he wrote, "The depression has hurt our work. We need help badly. Depending, as the mission work does, upon contributions, as people's incomes fell off, the gifts to the work did also."

Despite this, he courageously quoted a motto which had long inspired him: "Everything worth while in the world has been accomplished notwithstanding." He sensed that God is still on the throne, guiding through difficult times as well as through those when life flows smoothly.

In the early thirties, numerous volunteers came to his aid, as in other years, when such help had meant much to his Labrador success. By the thousands interested men and women took up his cause and made it their own. Students on summer vacations traveled to his country where they worked in the various enterprises. No task was too disagreeable or difficult for them to perform. Others in England, Canada and the United States assisted in selling the goods produced by the Labradorians, and friends were liberal in giving money, sending clothes, supplying boats or whatever else was needed. God laid Grenfell's needs upon the hearts of the English-speaking world, and those needs were eagerly supplied.

Benefits were given by various organizations, chief among which was the annual benefit at the Metropolitan Opera House in New York City, which secured from five to nine thousand dollars for Labrador.

An army of assistants flocked to his cause, of whom he said, "These young men and women have not despised any kind of work. They come as the sons and daughters of millionaires co-operating with those who have worked their way to Labrador." There were mathematicians, surgeons, engineers, architects, lawyers, army officers, librarians, teachers, nurses and debutantes.

Dr. Grenfell was sincerely grateful for this co-operation and gave credit liberally to these volunteers for much that had been done in the Labradorian wilderness. "But for my splendid colleagues and helpers on the coast and off it, our work would have died years ago," he said.

Few missionary enterprises enlisted such wholehearted and enthusiastic support from so many as did his work. Dr. Grenfell was able to convince people of his own sincerity and genuine Christianity, and hence they came forward willingly with their money and lives to further the cause.

As the years slipped by, the doctor found that he must relinquish some of his strenuous activities. "The young people must carry on. I will do what I can to help," he said. He was forced to give up dog-team driving and the hazardous summer cruises, while he found that he could more profitably devote his energies and remaining years to raising funds, supervising activities, planning future work and writing. As a world personage, beloved by all, there was a steady demand for him to speak, write articles for the press, and present Labrador's needs to the public.

When 1934 came, his physicians demanded that he leave Labrador and seek an easier life, for his health was precarious. Going to his Vermont home with his beloved Anne, who had shared his triumphs and now was to stand in the valley of the shadow of death with him, he went into semi-retirement. But Labrador was still in his heart, and he could not cease to work for that land so dear to him.

When the Italian-Ethiopian war broke out, he was saddened to see the Labradorian fish market disappear, and fish was essential to the life of his people. Genoa, Naples and Sicilian cities were the chief ports to which the fish were shipped, but the difficulties of delivering the goods were increased by the war. More serious, credit could not wisely be extended to Italian firms.

Although in the middle and late thirties Dr. Grenfell was no longer physically active, he was still a leading figure in Newfoundland, and was suggested to fill the post of governor of Newfoundland when the island should be controlled by a commission. This was an honor which he could not accept, however, for Christ had called him to Labrador as a physician for the bodies and souls of the people.

Great sorrow came to the missionary when Anne, known the world over as Lady Grenfell, went to be with the Lord on December 9, 1938. This was an irreparable loss to the doctor, for she had been a beloved companion, an untiring associate on whom he leaned, a business partner who had taken much of the load off his shoulders.

"Now that the final goal seems not so far away," he wrote shortly before her death, "we are holding hands closer than ever, confident that the final experience of life also will be easier to face then, and indeed become another joyous adventure, when these worn-out bodily machines of ours shall be discarded, and on the other side we shall work again in new fields together."

Not many more years passed before he joined his be-

loved in that Land of Celestial Delight. Yet even during
that little time he was active in Christ's service. He must
be true to his vision of the Master, of whom he wrote in
his book *What Christ Means to Me*:

"Christ ever meant to me a peerless Leader, whose challenge was not to save ourselves, but to lose ourselves; not to
understand Him, but to have courage to follow Him . . .
treading in the footsteps of Christ explains the meaning of
life."

The year after Anne's death, accompanied by her ashes,
he arrived on August 31, 1939, at the St. Anthony pier,
the first visit he had made there since his retirement in
1934. Because of a serious heart ailment, he had been
ordered by his physicians to stay in Vermont. Each summer before her death he had planned to return to the mission and revel again in the glorious scenes which had
claimed so many of his years, but the doctors would not
permit him to do so.

He was greeted at the pier by old friends, former patients, Labradorians, assistants, with whom he had spent
many thrilling and adventure-packed days. A welcoming
arch had been built across the pier by his friends, and
he was escorted under the arch by his daughter Rosamond.
He was welcomed by Dr. S. C. Curtis, chief of the St.
Anthony hospital, and medical superintendent of all Grenfell missions.

On the following day, when Anne's final wish to be
buried in Labrador had been fulfilled, a glorious and impressive funeral service was held, and Lady Grenfell's
ashes were deposited in a specially prepared stone vault,
high on a hill overlooking the mission site. With weary
steps the missionary doctor walked back from the hillock
and down to the St. Anthony home, where for a short time
he enjoyed the familiar scenes and then returned to his
home, Kinlock House, in Charlotte, Vermont.

He could not rest. He must be active in planning for the

mission's future. Back at Kinlock House, he mapped out a program of expansion, and Christian progress for Labrador's many ventures. During the morning of October 10, 1940, he had been busy in his room, and when afternoon came, he played a game of croquet, as he often did. On returning to his room, he took up the unfinished program on which he was working for the Grenfell Association, but the Master he so dearly loved called him home, and peacefully he fell asleep in Jesus. The service-filled life had come to an end. The Christ Dr. Grenfell had served so faithfully had said, "Well done, thou good and faithful servant . . . enter thou into the joy of thy Lord."

The work he accomplished in Labrador is a monument to this man whose first aim was to serve Christ, and whose life-purpose was to heal, in the Master's Name, those sick in body and soul.

Funeral services for Dr. Grenfell were held in Boston, and many famous people were present, including representatives of the English government. There was but one spot suited to receive his ashes—the cold bleak land to which he had literally given his heart. His body was cremated, and the following year the ashes were taken to St. Anthony, where they were buried beside Lady Grenfell's under a gray boulder on the hillside.

And now the cold northern winds blow over them— winds which they braved to bring Christ, the Healer of bodies and the Redeemer of souls to Labrador.

Printed in the U.S.A.